Catching Diamonds

By

R. E. M. Holland

Contents

Dedications

Dedicated to my Family & Friends who remain supportive.

Dedications are hidden within the pages.

And

Special Dedications here to my

Mother, Sisters, Nana, Grandma, and CJ

for their continued love and support.

Acknowledgments

I probably would not have had the dedication to complete this project

had it not been for my family and friends. A special thanks to my Mom

for working as my agent and finding a publisher. And a huge thank

you to ~ ~ ~ ~ Publishing Company ~~ ~ ~. And a super special thanks

to my Great Aunt Nancy (who is a tremendous writer in her own right)

for taking the time to tackle this project and edit it for me.

Dear Reader,

I understand that in the "real world", the college world series is held in Omaha, Nebraska, and played with double eliminations. I also understand that the "real world" brackets are different. I separated my brackets into a Northern and Southern Division and removed double eliminations out of pure simplicity. I understand that I may have avid sports fans who read this novel and would want answers to those questions. Likewise, I understand that I may have readers who know nothing about baseball and are here for the story. Because of this, I felt that differences should be met in the middle; so, I created a fictitious world where the sports division is split two ways and follows a similar play-off bracket to the MLB.

Thank you for your understanding and support. I hope you enjoy <u>Catching Diamonds.</u>

~ ~ R.E.M. Holland

"There may be people that have more talent than you,

but there's no excuse for anyone

to work harder than you do."

~ ~ Derek Jeter

PROLOGUE

"Marcus! Marcus! Marcus!" The crowd at Anthem University in El Paso, Texas was going crazy. It was a bright, sunny day, the sky was clear blue and ninety-eight degrees. It was also the first time in college history that the school's baseball team was one win away from competing for the National Championship. The excitement was genuine and real!

"I'm putting J.B. in as your catcher," Coach Kozlowski told Marcus as he was sitting on the bench preparing for the day's big game. Coach Kozlowski was a small man, balding, and had a thick white mustache. He was in his early fifties and had a crooked nose from a break when he was younger. He had served as head baseball coach for Anthem for twenty years but was never able to coach the team to the championships.

Marcus looked up at his coach and said, "Out of all the years I have played baseball, I have never been as nervous as I am right now."

"Being nervous is part of the game, plus it shows your human side. There's nothing wrong with emotions, Marcus," Coach Kozlowski replied.

Marcus nodded in agreement and said, "I just don't want to let anyone down."

"Marcus," said Coach Kozlowski. "Out of everyone I have ever coached, you are, by far, the best pitcher to step foot on the pitching mound at Anthem University. Regardless of whether we win or lose, all that matters is that you try, keep your heart in the right place, and keep your love for the game."

J.B. abruptly came around the corner and slapped Marcus on the shoulder. J.B. was shorter than Marcus, but average height, dark hair, and typically sported a five o'clock shadow. His catching gear made him look larger than he really was, which was a good thing because other teams would recognize him as a power hitter, and a threat at the plate.

"Great news! I'm catching up for you today," J.B. told Marcus. "Now let's get out there and win us a game." Marcus laughed and said, "You got it, Bud!"

Marcus and J.B. were told it was almost time for the game to start, so they started to walk out onto the field. As Marcus and J.B. took their places behind the plate, and on the mound, the stadium started to fill with cheers of "Marcus! Marcus!" Students and families were overjoyed to see their team play for a chance to make the National Championship playoffs. Marcus began to warm up as the rest of the team took their positions on the field.

Marcus Fjord was one of the top pitchers in all of college baseball. It was said that his curveball was practically unhittable, and his fastball was so fast, you could hear the snap of leather on J.B.'s glove, even over the cheering crowd. In Marcus's first year at Anthem University, he broke the record for most strikeouts in a single season. This, however, was Marcus's one and only chance at a National Championship due to his senior year. Marcus won every honor that the college offered for baseball. He was the proud recipient of "Player of the Year" for the last three years. He won Anthem's Golden Glove Award his sophomore year, and he won Anthem's Silver Slugger Award the prior season. Each year Marcus' skills increased exponentially. The only thing that eluded Marcus was The National Championship.

As the game started, the home plate umpire yelled "Play Ball!" Marcus found his confidence. He struck out the first six batters on eighteen pitches. Four batters went down swinging while two went down looking. Marcus was a force to be reckoned with. Marcus entered the sixth inning with twelve strikeouts and threw a perfect game. The score was still zero to zero, as the sixth inning began. Marcus threw a fastball to the first batter, and he hit it on the ground to the shortstop, who scooped it up and threw it to first for the out. The next batter struck out swinging. The third batter of the inning worked a full count. Three balls and two strikes. Marcus and J.B. both knew that if Marcus threw one more ball it would walk a runner onto first and blow his perfect game. J.B. gave the signal for Marcus to throw his best pitch, the curveball. Marcus nodded in agreement, wound up, and released. To the batter, it appeared that Marcus had just thrown a fastball right through the center of the plate. The batter's eyes grew as big as saucers, and he swung with all his might. At the last second, the ball swept down, and the batter struck out swinging. At that, the crowd went wild with "Marcus" chants! After Marcus pitched the sixth inning, he began to feel a tightness in his elbow, while he sat on the bench. He wrapped his arm in a warm compress, despite the ninety-eight-degree summer temperature, and he was sweating profusely. While Marcus watched his team bat in the bottom of the sixth, he continued to treat his elbow. Suddenly, he heard a loud crack and looked up to see that J.B. had just hit the go-ahead homerun. After the home run, the crowd jumped to their feet, waving their arms in the air, and started chanting "J.B.! J.B.!"

Marcus returned to the mound in the top of the seventh inning knowing he was only nine outs away from pitching a perfect game and advancing his team to the championship playoffs. Even with the tightness in his elbow, Marcus continued to mow batters down. When the top of the ninth inning approached, the score was still one to nothing, and Marcus was three outs away from pitching a perfect game. The first batter Marcus faced swung and missed a curveball, but hit the second pitch, a fastball, up into the air. The centerfielder took chase. The ball was heading for the outfield grass at amazing speed. If the ball hit the ground, that would be the end of the perfect game. The Center Fielder leapt and dove for the ball making a spectacular catch. Relieved, "only two outs left," Marcus thought.

The next batter worked a full count. Marcus threw three balls, and then two consecutive fastballs that the batter swung at and missed. Again, Marcus found himself in a situation where one more ball would blow his perfect game. Marcus and J.B. both agreed that the next pitch would be a changeup. Marcus got his footing, wound up, and released. The change of speed made the batter swing early, and miss. Marcus only needed one more out to complete his perfect game and advance his team to the playoffs. The next batter that came to the plate was the other team's best hitter and had a five hundred average against Marcus. When J.B. saw that he would be pinch-hitting, he called time out so he could talk to Marcus. When J.B. got back behind the plate, he gave the signal for Marcus to throw his curveball. Marcus nodded in agreement, wiped the sweat from his brow and eyes, and got his footing. This batter was also short and stocky, which changed the strike zone. Marcus made the needed adjustment, wound up, and released the pitch. As soon as the pitch left his fingers, Marcus felt something in his elbow snap. The pain was so excruciating that Marcus immediately fell to the dirt in agony. Meanwhile, the pitch curved and was hit right into the third baseman's glove. Marcus had thrown a perfect game and advanced his team to the playoffs, but the crowd was silent watching Marcus writhing in pain on the ground! J.B. and Coach Kozlowski ran to the mound to check on their star player. Marcus painfully exclaimed what happened, and Coach Kozlowski called for their athletic trainer, Mervin to evaluate the injury. After several minutes, Mervin determined that Marcus needed to be rushed to the hospital, immediately!

Coach Kozlowski, J.B., and the rest of the team followed the ambulance to the hospital and waited to hear what the doctor would say. Marcus was their best pitcher, and nobody knew what they would do if they were told that Marcus would not be allowed to play in the playoffs.

There was a knock on the door, and Doctor Sanders entered. He was the best orthopedic doctor and surgeon in the area. Doctor Sanders was in his early fifties and had a comely face, grey hair, and blue eyes.

"I have some harsh news," Dr. Sanders said. "It seems that you have torn the ligament in your elbow. Now, this is not uncommon among pitchers. We will need to perform "Tommy John" surgery to repair the elbow. If all goes as planned, you should be back on the pitching mound within a year."

With that statement, Marcus's hopes of leading his team to their first National Championship were crushed!

As Marcus was recovering from successful "Tommy John" surgery, there was a knock on the door, and J.B. and Coach Kozlowski entered the hospital room. Marcus was still slightly drowsy from the anesthesia but painfully sat upright to hear the news.

"Did you guys win the playoffs?" Marcus asked hopefully.

"Well," said Coach, "we are all winners in a sense, but unfortunately, we lost the game."

Marcus was filled with grief, and through his sorrow, he apologized.

"It's not your fault, so don't apologize," J.B. told Marcus. "We all messed up, and we learn from our mistakes."

Coach quickly interjected. "Remember, winning or losing doesn't define who we are, how we handle ourselves after such wins or losses is the key. The fact that we lost means nothing, but the fact that we showed grace after a huge loss like this...now that means *everything!*"

Suddenly, there was another knock on the door, and Dr. Sanders entered. "Marcus, I have good and bad news. Would you like me to return so we may discuss this in private?" Dr. Sanders asked. Marcus answered quickly and said, "No, J.B. and Coach are like family. They can stay. You can speak freely in front of them."

"Very well," Dr. Sanders replied. "The good news is that the surgery was a success. However, the bad news is that the tear in your elbow was much worse than we had originally anticipated. It is my professional opinion that it would be unwise to continue playing baseball. It would only be a matter of time until your arm would suffer permanent damage. I'm sorry."

Marcus was in complete shock.   After all his achievements on the diamond, how could someone tell him that he would never be able to play the sport he loved so much? Playing baseball was as easy as breathing to him. He was on the verge of tears when Coach said, "Well, there's always coaching."

Chapter 1

The bell rang indicating the end of the school day. Nevaeh Bennet was fourteen years old, and almost done with her freshman year of High School. She had long brown hair that she often kept in a ponytail, brown eyes, and braces. Nevaeh left her last-period English class and searched the halls for her best friend, Rachel Sullivan. Nevaeh was average height for a girl, which would frequently make finding Rachel in crowds difficult. Rachel was a lot shorter than average girls, which made finding her a lot more difficult in large crowds. Sometimes Nevaeh wished she was taller, to make finding Rachel easier. The only thing that helped Nevaeh locate Rachel in these situations was Rachel's bright red curly hair. Finally, after five minutes of searching Nevaeh spotted Rachel.

"Rachel!" Nevaeh yelled.

Rachel jumped as Nevaeh grabbed her bookbag. "Why can't you ever calmly get my attention? You know I spook easily," Rachel said.

Nevaeh smiled and said, "Well, If I didn't startle you, there would be no fun in finding you. Plus, there's no time for calm. Today is the day Coach Walker is posting the list of names of people who made the baseball team."

Rachel stopped dead in her tracks and looked at Nevaeh nervously. "What?"

"Why are you stopping and looking at me like that?" Nevaeh snapped.

Rachel timidly responded and said, "It's nothing, but what if..."

"...if I don't make the team because I'm a girl?" Nevaeh asked harshly.

"Well, to be honest, yeah. I mean, I know how good of a player you are and how hard you have worked with your dad at catching but..." Rachel grew hesitant and did not want to finish her statement.

"Well, but what?" Nevaeh asked.

Rachel hesitated a little longer but finally said, "There has never been a girl on the baseball team, and Vinny is a good catcher too. Don't you think Coach Walker will choose him first?"

"He might, but I'm better at catching so that would be sexist," Nevaeh said. Rachel looked at her and said, "Maybe so, but even if you do make the team, and Vinny does too, won't your little crush on him distract you?"

Nevaeh was quick to answer. "**Nothing** will distract me. I mean, yeah, Vinny is cute, but he is also a giant jerk. I've worked too hard for this, and I won't let Coach Walker or Vinny Green stop me from achieving my goals."

Finally, Nevaeh and Rachel reached the list of names that was posted on the bulletin board outside of the Gymnasium. When Nevaeh got to the front of the line, she ran her fingers down the list searching for her name. She saw Vinny Green's name on the list, but she couldn't find her own. She looked again, and again with the same results. Nevaeh began to get frustrated, and tears formed in her eyes.

"Why didn't Coach Walker pick me?" Nevaeh asked in a sad voice. "There must be a good reason," Rachel insisted. "It can't be because of your gender, that *would* make him sexist like you said."

"Well, let's go and find out then," and with that, Neveah burst into the gymnasium and headed straight for Coach Walker's office. Neveah was very outgoing, and when she had her heart set on something, she meant to have it. Nevaeh knocked on Coach Walker's door, and heard him say "Come in."

Coach Walker was a tall man with a muscular build. He was in his mid-forties. His hair was black but had a few gray hairs peeking through. He also kept his face clean-shaven which showed a scar above his lip from a fishing accident when he was younger. All the students like to make rumors about how he got his scar, but Coach Walker told all his physical education classes each year about how his older brother caught him instead of a fish during that summer fishing trip.

"Ah, Ms. Bennet. To what do I owe this pleasure?" Coach Walker asked as Nevaeh opened the door and took a seat in his office.

Nevaeh wasted no time, was blunt, and straight to the point. "Why did you cut me from the team?" she asked.

Coach Walker sighed and said, "Nevaeh, you are undoubtedly very talented. In fact, you may very well be one of the best catchers I have ever seen, but I think your talents would be better suited on the softball field rather than the baseball diamond."

"I don't understand." Nevaeh snapped. "It's basically the exact same sport except one used a giant yellow ball, and the other a smaller white one."

Coach Walker sighed again and said, "Nevaeh, I understand your frustrations, but my decision stands. I can talk to Coach Fisher about finding you a spot on the softball team. Would you like that?"

Before Nevaeh could answer, there was a knock on Coach Walker's door and Vinny Green entered the room. Vincent, whom everyone called Vinny, was a boy in the same grade as Nevaeh and Rachel. He had blonde hair that wasn't long, but it wasn't short either. A lot of girls in their grade had a crush on him, and even though Nevaeh was one of those girls, she still thought he was a huge jerk. She had no problem admitting that his eyes were perfect pools of blue, his teeth were perfect, and he was athletically fit. But still, she thought he was a jerk, nonetheless.

Vinny mocked, "Is little Ms. Nevaeh Bennet upset that I was chosen to be the starting catcher on our baseball team? I don't even know why Coach let you try out. Girls belong on the softball field, not on a baseball diamond," he snarled.

Nevaeh shot right back, "I'll have you know that softball is also played on a diamond, so stop calling it a field. Secondly, girls can do anything boys can do, and I guarantee I'm a better catcher than you."

Vinny snorted, "I'd sooner be the King of England before you play ball better than me."

Nevaeh was so frustrated she began to turn beet red. Before Nevaeh could lash back, Coach Walker stood and said, "I'm going home for the day, and I will have no more of this talk. Now hurry along and get home."

Nevaeh had never felt so frustrated, and she thought of a few choice words but decided to bite her tongue rather than call Vinny and Coach Walker sexist. Rachel was waiting in the hallway for Nevaeh.

"Well, how did that go?" Rachel asked.

Before Nevaeh had a chance to explain what happened inside Coach Walker's office, she received a text message from her dad. "Where are you? I've been waiting outside," the text read. "I'm on my way now," Nevaeh messaged back.

"My Dad is waiting outside," Nevaeh told Rachel. "I'll call you tonight plus I need to cool off anyway." Nevaeh and Rachel parted ways, and Nevaeh got in the car with her dad.

Chapter 2

"Why do you have Mom's car?" Nevaeh asked her dad. "Took the truck to the shop," her dad responded. "How was school, kiddo?"

Nevaeh's father was a bald man, as bald as an egg, some would say. He let his beard grow like a caveman, and he started to put on some pounds. He used to be athletically fit, but over the years, he let his sweet tooth take over. Jason Bennet was the foreman for the local lumber yard, "Lucky's Lumber" and always wore the green cap with the double "L" logo.

"I hate mom's car. The air conditioning is broken and it's a thousand degrees out," Nevaeh said as she rolled down the passenger window. "And school was fine up until Coach Walker posted the baseball list."

Mr. Bennet sighed. "Let me guess, Walker cut you from the team, huh? Do you remember what I told you?"

Mr. Bennet was always telling Nevaeh things, but in this instance, she remembered his advice word for word. "Expect the worst, so you won't be disappointed. Coach Walker is a man set in old-school ways, and probably won't allow a girl on his coveted baseball team." "It's not fair, and things should be different. Just because I'm a female, it doesn't mean I can't play baseball as good, if not better than a male," Nevaeh exclaimed.

Her father looked sad and emphasized, "Unfortunately, to some men, and I disagree, but to some men, a woman's place is in the kitchen, not on a diamond." "Yeah, and we're only expected to wear their precious diamonds on our fingers, and cook, and clean for them. It's ridiculous, and degrading," Nevaeh lamented.

As they drove past their local diner, "The Moonlit Rose", Nevaeh asked if they could stop for food, or at the very least, a milkshake.

"Your mother is making pork chops that should be finished by the time we get home, and a milkshake would ruin your appetite," Mr. Bennet said.

Nevaeh was already frustrated from her encounter with Vinny, and Coach Walker, so she said, "I hate pork chops!" and stuck her arm out of the window to catch the air.

"Put your arm back in the car!" Mr. Bennet roared. "The last thing I need is you smacking a mailbox and snapping your arm off! Your mother would kill me, and you would never be able to play baseball."

"OH MY GOD!!" Nevaeh yelled. "Can you ever stop harping on me for once? Every time I have a bad day, people tell me what I can do, and what I'm not allowed to do because I'm a girl. We can't even stop for real food. Pork chops are disgusting! It's always nag, nag, nag from you and mom. Do your homework, help your sister, do the dishes! Nag, nag, nag..."

... "ENOUGH!!" yelled Mr. Bennet. "I have done nothing to you to deserve this attitude, and I am your father! I will NOT be spoken to in this manner by my own daughter. I understand that you are frustrated but taking your frustrations out on me over pork chops is not a wise choice. When we get home, you will go straight to your room, and think about this little outburst of yours!"

"Pork chops are not why I'm upset," Nevaeh yelled crying. "You don't understand anything about me! And I'm not eating the pork chops!"

Mr. Bennet only smiled and said, "Well, I guess you will be going to bed hungry then."

Nevaeh looked at her father, tears rolling down her cheeks, and yelled "Sometimes you can be so dense. Sometimes I wish I had a different dad!"

Before Mr. Bennet could respond, Nevaeh saw bright lights, heard the screech of tires, and everything went black.

Chapter 3

Beep, Beep, Beep...the sound sent jolts of pain through her head. Nevaeh lay there with her eyes closed. There was no sound except for the constant beep. She felt a tingle and pain in her right arm.

"Where am I?" she thought. "What happened?" She tried to use her right arm to sit up, but the attempt caused her severe agony, and she couldn't move. Nevaeh opened her eyes, looked around, and saw that she was in a hospital room surrounded by beautiful flowers and get-well cards. Her arm continued to ache, and when she looked at her arm, she almost passed out from shock. Where her arm should have been, Nevaeh found only a stump where her elbow and forearm used to be. The stump was wrapped in white gauze and a ton of bandages. Nevaeh could still feel her fingers even though they were gone. She began to sob, and her silent sobs soon turned into hysterical crying. "Any minute now I'll wake up from this nightmare and I'll have my arm," she kept thinking. The sound of Nevaeh's hyperventilating got the attention of her mother and sister. Katie and Morgan Bennet came rushing into the hospital room, to Nevaeh's bedside. Katie Bennet was Nevaeh's mom and worked at the local pharmacy. She had curly brown hair, brown eyes, and a comely face. Morgan was Nevaeh's little sister. She was ten years old and looked very much like a mini-Nevaeh. Their biggest difference was that Morgan loved to wear dresses, paint her nails, have sleepovers, and have tea parties. Whereas Nevaeh would rather be outside getting dirty, watching horror movies, or playing sports.

"Mom, what happened to my arm?" Nevaeh cried.

Mrs. Bennet took Nevaeh's remaining hand into her own and said, "Oh sweetie, I'm so sorry." Tears started to form in her eyes. "There was a terrible accident. As your father was passing an intersection, a drunk driver ran the stop sign and crashed into the side of the car. Your arm was out of the window at the time and was trapped in the wreckage. Doctor Sanders saved what he could, but he had to remove your arm from the elbow down. The damage was too extensive, too severe. I'm so sorry sweetie."

Nevaeh couldn't hold back her tears. She was more than devastated. Suddenly, she realized that her dad was not in the room, and she noticed a sadness in her mother and her sister's eyes.

"Mom, where's dad?" she asked hesitantly. She feared that she already knew the answer. Tears began to fall from Mrs. Bennet's and Morgan's eyes as if they were waterfalls, and Nevaeh knew the answer before Morgan responded. When Morgan cried, "Our dad's dead," Nevaeh felt retching in the pit of her stomach. She suddenly felt lightheaded, as if she was going to puke and pass out all at the same time. How could she lose her arm, and her father at the same moment? Mrs. Bennet quickly interjected and said, "Doctor Sanders did everything he could, but your father's injuries were too devastating. There was no way he could have survived."

Nevaeh lay in her hospital bed, shocked at having only one arm and looking at her mother and sister in total disbelief. "Any second I will wake up, and this will all be a horrible nightmare," she thought. She pinched her leg to be sure, and that was when she realized this was no dream, but a harsh and cruel reality.

"I don't understand," Nevaeh said. "How could God be so cruel?" she thought. Her family attended church each and every Sunday. She wondered what she did to deserve this punishment.

Everyone sat in silence to process what had happened.

"I'm not going to give up," Nevaeh said suddenly. Her mother and sister were confused. They looked at each other, then at her. Finally, her mom asked, "Giving up on what, sweetie?"

Nevaeh looked at her arm, and then at her mom and said, "Dad would never give up, and I won't either. He believed in me when no one else would. He taught me everything I know about baseball. Arm or no arm, I'm bound and determined to be one of the greatest players to ever step foot on a diamond."

Don't you think that's going to be impossible?" Morgan asked bluntly. Their mother put her hand up to avoid an argument from happening and said, "Nothing is impossible when you set your mind to it. Your father would be proud of you."

Nevaeh was still emotional when she remembered the argument she had with her father over pork chops. "I hope he will be proud of me. I didn't mean those awful things I said," she thought.

"Mom, Dad, and I had an argument before the accident, and I said some pretty harsh things. Nevaeh fought back tears as she asked, "Do you think he can forgive me, and know that I still love him?"

"Of course, he can forgive you, sweetie" her mom replied, "and he knows you loved him. Always remember that he loved you too."

There was a sudden knock on the door and a nurse entered with more flowers, and a get well soon card. "These just arrived, so I brought them right up," the nurse said, smiling. "Thank you very much," Nevaeh replied.

The nurse handed the card to Nevaeh and placed the flowers by the window. As the nurse was leaving, Morgan asked Nevaeh who the card was from. With much difficulty and some assistance from her mom, Nevaeh opened the card and said, "I don't know, it isn't signed."

Morgan bit her lip and then said, "That's weird. Anyway, what's it say?" Nevaeh read the writing inside the card aloud. "In times of struggle, remember to keep your faith. My heart breaks for your physical and emotional loss. Stay strong and remember that how you handle yourself during difficult times will define who you are, and who you are meant to become. Do not allow anyone to tell you what you can and cannot do. Follow your heart, and you will achieve greatness. I expect to see you on a baseball diamond one day. Here's to wishing you a speedy recovery, and great health."

"It's a shame they didn't sign it," her mother said. "Such kind words, and beautiful flowers."

"They are nice flowers, and the card is nice too" Nevaeh agreed. "I just wish I knew who they were from."

Chapter 4

The following week, the Bennet family celebrated the life of Jason Bennet, and sadly, laid him to rest. Before the burial, the family allowed calling hours at the funeral home. A lot of people attended to pay their respects. In fact, there were so many people that a line formed out the door and wrapped around the building. Nevaeh never realized how many people her dad knew. She knew most of the people from town, and Lucky's Lumber, but there were still several people she had never seen before. A lot of people shared stories and memories that made her laugh, and cry. One story from an old college friend about Jason being chased by an ostrich that got loose when they went to the zoo made Nevaeh and Morgan laugh especially hard. When it came time for the family to speak, Nevaeh volunteered, having only been released from the hospital a couple of days before. Nevaeh stood up, her arm still wrapped in lots of bandages, and walked to the podium. As she stood at the podium, she was surrounded by flowers of all colors. Her father lay in a casket behind her, and behind him were large windows. The sunlight shone through, and before she could speak, someone in the crowd said, "Oh my, she looks so beautiful." Nevaeh had on a light blue dress, and this was an occasion where she did her makeup and let her hair flow. She heard someone else comment on how she looked like an angel. Nevaeh did not plan a speech, so she just started talking.

"Hello everyone." There were a lot more people than she thought when she looked out into the crowd and saw everyone looking back at her. She paused, took a deep breath, and continued.

"My name is Nevaeh Bennet. I heard someone mention that I look like an angel, and I wanted to say thank you for that. My father named me Nevaeh because it is heaven-spelled backward. I was his firstborn, so he always called me his little angel, and now *he* is my angel."

She paused, then proceeded to say, "I came up here to tell you all how great of a man my father was, but when I look out and see all of your faces, I know that you already know that. However, I do want to share how my father had never given up on me, or my sister, Morgan. I can imagine it would be incredibly hard for a father to have two completely different daughters, and support them both, nonetheless. I will always cherish and remember our times in the backyard playing catch." Nevaeh paused, looked at the bulletin board of pictures that were placed by the flowers, and plucked a picture off.

"This is my favorite picture of me and my dad. We were on vacation in New York City, and he took me to the Bronx to see the Yankees play the Boston Red Sox. We took this picture after Aaron Judge hit a home run. We were sitting in the "Judge's Chambers" Section. We were both so happy! Everyone knows how great of a man he was, but only Morgan and I can tell you how great of a father he was. He loved us something fierce, and our mother, too." Nevaeh turned and looked at the casket. Tears started to roll down her cheeks. "Dad, you would never give up on me. When I wanted to quit, you always supported me knowing I would come back. I wish you could come back and teach me how to play with one arm. Even though you are gone, you will always remain in my heart. I love you and I miss you so much. I promise I will make you proud."

Chapter 5

Three years after Nevaeh lost her arm and her father, she still struggled to adapt, having only one arm. Before the accident Nevaeh was right-handed, so playing baseball and getting through school became a challenge. Even completing the simple task of writing her own name was difficult. Nevaeh never gave up, and as time progressed, she learned to accommodate her disability. Learning to play catcher with only one arm had proved to be the most difficult task of all. Even though she already knew how to play the position, she basically had to relearn. Playing with one arm proved to be largely different than playing with two. Catching wasn't the only struggle either. She had to learn to bat with only her non-dominant hand and arm. Her right arm had finally healed, and she completed physical therapy the summer before her senior year of high school. Since her father was gone, she was forced to practice with Morgan in the backyard, even though Morgan wanted nothing to do with sports. Morgan also couldn't throw the ball far enough if her life depended on it. Although, with Morgan's horrible throwing, Nevaeh's blocking skills increased. But that was the only skill that was increasing.

"I need you to actually get the ball to me," Nevaeh told Morgan multiple times. Nevaeh was trying to learn how to catch the ball, toss it up, drop the glove, and grab the ball to throw it.

She needed to learn to do this as fluently as possible if she was ever going to be a starting catcher.

"Why do you even need to learn all of that?" Morgan would ask. "Well, if I'm the catcher in the game, and a runner on first tries to steal second after the pitch, I need to try to throw them out," Nevaeh replied. A lot of the time Nevaeh would start to doubt herself. "No matter how hard I work, I will never be a starting catcher," she would think.

Ever since the accident almost three years ago, Nevaeh has suffered from depression. Whenever she would get sad, she would talk herself out of it. "You can't give up! You won't give up" she thought. Her depression started to disappear mid-way through summer when Vinny Green rang the doorbell, handed her flowers, and asked her out on a date. At first, Nevaeh thought it was some kind of cruel joke. She said "no" and slammed the door in his face. Vinny was persistent though and rang the doorbell again. Eventually, Nevaeh said she would go out with him, but if it was some joke, she promised she would break his nose.

Nevaeh loved horror movies, so they went to the movie Plex and watched "The Night the Dead Walked" which was about zombies. Vinny bought the collectible popcorn buckets which were shaped like zombie heads, candy, and large sodas for each of them. After the movie, they drove to the Moonlit Rose for dinner. Vinny had borrowed his dad's Ford Mustang for the date. It was all black except for the red stripe going down the center of the hood. Nevaeh loved how those colors meshed, but never commented on them. Throughout the night, Vinny had been a complete gentleman. He even got out of the car, ran around, and opened Nevaeh's door for her when they got to the Moonlit Rose.

"Why isn't he being a jerk like usual?" she thought to herself. When they entered the diner, there was a sign that read, "Please seat yourself" so they chose the booth in the corner by the jukebox.

The Moonlit Rose was an old-fashioned diner modeled after the popular diners from the late 1950s and 1960s. The floor was checkered black and white, and all the booths had red seats, or stools at the counter. All the waitresses wore red dresses with white aprons, and they were always very kind. The Moonlit Rose was popular in the area and known all over for its famous homemade ice cream and milkshakes. The waitress came to the table, handed them menus, and took their drink orders. Nevaeh and Vinny both ordered a nice cold glass of root beer. They looked over their menus in silence, and when Nevaeh looked up at Vinny after deciding what she wanted to eat, she found him looking at her.

"What?" she asked.

Vinny blushed and said, "Nothing, you just look really pretty."

"Thank you!" Nevaeh replied. "It's taken me forever to master a hairbrush and tie up my hair one-handed. The first couple of months were torture. I struggled to brush my teeth and tie my shoes. Basically, I struggled with every normal task. Try cooking one-handed or taking off bottle caps."

Vinny laughed, "I can't even imagine."

The waitress returned with their root beers and took their order. Nevaeh ordered a regular cheeseburger and fries, and Vinny ordered the BBQ bacon cheeseburger and fries, his favorite.

"Do you remember our freshman year when I told you that I would be the King of England before you would play better ball than me?" Vinny quizzed Nevaeh. "And here comes Vinny, the Jerk," she thought. "Yeah..." she said hesitantly.

"Well, I guess I'll be becoming the King of England soon," Vinny said. Nevaeh looked at him and said, "What do you mean by that?"

"It's just, that I've noticed how hard you keep working to be a catcher. Had it been me in your situation, I would have quit by now," Vinny admitted.

Nevaeh never expected Vinny Green, of all people, to respect her determination. Plus, he's been nice to her the entire evening. Finally, she asked bluntly, "Why have you been so nice tonight? Any other time you're being a jerk or pretending like I don't exist."

"I always knew you existed, and that's why I was being a jerk. I know it sounds stupid, but I was always mean to you because I had a crush on you, and I was jealous of your talent behind the plate," Vinny admitted. "When you were in the accident, I was so scared," Vinny admitted. "I even prayed for you."

Nevaeh was shocked! "That was unexpected..." Then she laughed. Vinny laughed too and said, "If the truth be told, I had a crush on you since the third grade. I just didn't think you liked me, so I played it off like I didn't like you. I should have treated you with more respect. I'm so sorry!" Vinny apologized, sheepishly.

Nevaeh accepted his apology and the two of them cleared their dinner trash and ordered two famous chocolate shakes before leaving. When Vinny dropped Nevaeh off at home, he got out of the Mustang and walked her to the door like a gentleman. She thanked him for an amazing evening and turned to go inside, but Vinny caught her wrist. "Wait..." he said. Nevaeh turned back to look at Vinny, who had always been confident when she saw him, but he looked really nervous at the moment. And then she found out why.

"Will you be my girlfriend?" Vinny blurted out. Shocked, Nevaeh just stood there looking at him. Finally, she smiled, said "yes", very happily, and went inside to call Rachel.

Chapter 6

With the start of her Senior year looming, Nevaeh had a lot on her plate. She needed to balance her new boyfriend, academics, state testing requirements, college applications, and catching. She was determined to play softball at the very least during her last year of High School. She knew Coach Walker wouldn't let her on the baseball team, so she didn't want to waste her time. She was also thinking about the Senior Prom. The school year had yet to start, but she was still excited about the idea of prom with a boyfriend. Vinny was helping her regularly with catching, so she felt like she would definitely make the softball team. Tryouts would still be six months away, but Nevaeh looked at that as six months to improve her skills.

A week before the start of school, all students were required to meet with their school counselors to go over their schedules and make amendments. Nevaeh met with her counselor, Mrs. Matthews.

"It's so nice to see you," Mrs. Matthews greeted Nevaeh as she entered her office. "I have a surprise in your schedule that I think you'll enjoy. The district approved a new class this year. It is History of Baseball."

Mrs. Matthew was an extremely nice woman who cared deeply about all her students. She was also pleasingly plump. She wore large glasses that magnified her eyes and made her look like an owl. Her short curly brown hair also contributed to the owl effect. She usually wore very bright dresses that looked like tablecloths, but she was outgoing, and all the students loved her for that. Mrs. Matthews handed Nevaeh her schedule, and she looked it over.

First Semester: (Aug-Dec)
Second Semester (Jan-May)

Period 1-Astronomy-Mrs. Sherwin-Rm 170 1-Forensic Science-Mrs. Sherwin-Rm 170	Period
Period 2-Calculus-Mr. Yang-Rm 188 2-Calculus-Mr. Yang-Rm 188	Period
Period 3-English 12-Mr. Martin-Rm 216 3-English 12-Mr. Martin-Rm 216	Period
Period 4-PE-Mr. Walker-Gymnasium 4-PE-Mr. Walker-Gymnasium	Period
Period 5-Lunch-Cafeteria 5-Lunch-Cafeteria	Period
Period 6-History of Baseball. Walker-Gym 6-Painting II-Mrs. DeLine-Rm 172	Period
Period 7-Study Hall-Mrs. Sharp-Rm 167 7-Study Hall-Mrs. Sharp-Rm 167	Period
Period 8-World History 12-Mrs. Edwards-Rm 169 8-World History-Mrs. Edwards-Rm 169	Period

"I gave you Astronomy and Forensics to satisfy your science credit. Both are half-year courses. I signed you up for calculus for the Math credit. Obviously English and History are for their respective credits, as well as PE, and I signed you up for

History of Baseball and Painting Two since you took Painting One your freshman year for electives. Any objections?" Mrs. Matthews asked.

Nevaeh looked through her schedule, and said, "Everything looks good. English is my favorite class, and I hear Mr. Martin is awesome." Nevaeh bit her lip. "But is there any way that I can take PE and History of Baseball with a different teacher? And I'm not sure about Painting Two since I'm down an arm now."

Mrs. Matthews smiled and said, "I know that you have had your differences with Coach Walker in the past, but he is the only teacher available for History of Baseball, and I think it would do well for your future to work with someone with whom you've disagreed. He truly respects you, Nevaeh. This is an opportunity to grow and put these differences aside. As to Painting Two, I saw your work from Painting One and you are quite talented. If you can master catching and the use of a baseball bat, I'm sure you can handle a paintbrush. So, what do you say, Nevaeh? Will you give this schedule a try?"

Nevaeh thought, and quickly answered "Yes! It's a great opportunity for me."

I'm glad we can agree on that. Now before I let you go, let's talk colleges. I see you're signed up for the SATs, but have you applied to any colleges yet?" Mrs. Matthews asked.

"I've applied to four colleges. Three locals, and one in New York City. I sent applications to Texas Community College, Anthem University, Paramount University, and Elementz State College in New York", Nevaeh replied.

Mrs. Matthew's smiled wide. "Good! Good! Do you have a preference?" Nevaeh responded "I really want to stay local, but Elementz is a really good baseball college. I guess my preference would be Paramount. Anthem hasn't won any National Championships, but I'll go wherever I'm accepted," Nevaeh replied.

"Excellent!" Mrs. Matthews said clapping. "Be sure to keep me updated."

Once Nevaeh was dismissed from Mrs. Matthews's office, she ran home and called Rachel and Vinny to compare schedules. She called Rachel first because she knew she would probably be on the phone with Vinny longer. She was home alone, so she sat at the kitchen table, put her schedule in front of her, and called Rachel. Both girls got really excited when they found out that they had English, Astronomy, Forensics, Study Hall, and History together. "That means we are automatic partners for any projects," Nevaeh told Rachel.

Just as Nevaeh and Rachel finished their conversation, Morgan came home from her visit with Mrs. Matthews.

"How's your freshman year schedule look?" Nevaeh asked her little sister...who was growing up beautifully. "It sucks!" Morgan said pouting.

Nevach laughed. "I know, but each year it will get better, and you'll have more say in your schedule. Keep your head up."

"Yeah, great...but that doesn't help me now," Morgan lamented.

Nevaeh wanted some privacy to talk to Vinny, so she ran up to her room, kicked off her flip-flops, turned the fan on, and jumped on the bed. Nevaeh rolled onto her stomach, laid her schedule in front of her, and dialed Vinny's number. Nevaeh soon found that she had a History of Baseball, Calculus, and History with Vinny as well. "Awesome, I don't have to go through History of Baseball alone, and I get to spend the last period of the day with my boyfriend, AND best friend!" Nevaeh always got giddy when she talked to Vinny and couldn't stay still. She began to kick her legs but eventually got up and started to pace her room. They stayed on the phone until dinner was ready, but they continued to text until they fell asleep. Nevaeh went to bed that night thinking about how amazing her Senior year was going to be.

Chapter 7

The school year started on August 27th. Nevaeh found most of her classes to be easy. English was her favorite subject and Mr. Martin was awesome. He would act out scenes from books they were reading and even had different voices for all the characters. Mr. Martin had them thinking about their Senior paper topics early and told everyone to get a head start as it accounted for a large percentage of their overall grade. Currently, they were reading "Harry Potter" as a class which is where most of his acting and voices came from. They would be reading Shakespeare's "Hamlet" next. He kept telling them that "Hamlet" was a classic, and today's youth needed to value classic literature.

Astronomy mainly discussed the stars and planets, so that was fairly easy. Nevaeh also learned that there were three people who landed on the moon, and not just Neil Armstrong. Allen Shepherd and Buzz Aldrin also had that honor. She also found History to be incredibly easy, mainly because the answers could never change. Calculus was in between easy and hard. Some problems she could easily solve, while others were a bit more challenging. The two classes that she took with Coach Walker were polar opposites. PE was super easy, and Coach Walker paid her no attention. But the History of Baseball was incredibly difficult. She already struggled with the fact that she was the only girl in the class, and Coach Walker made her feel unwelcome. He would always call on her to answer his questions, even when she didn't raise her hand. Her only solitude was that Vinny was in the class with her. Still, even if she felt like she didn't belong, she still enjoyed the class and learned new things. They talked about MLB teams, and how their names used to be different, Lou Gehrig's disease, the curse of the great Bambino, and more. The class was hard, and she didn't like the teacher, but she was learning a lot.

As October came around, everything was still going smoothly for Nevaeh. She had straight A's in every subject. She even started to enjoy the History of Baseball and looked forward to learning new things. Nevaeh's sister, Morgan was not so thrilled about freshman year. Every time Nevaeh saw her in the hallway, she would look miserable, and ignore her.

"It's probably because of her friends," Nevaeh laughed and proceeded to her third-period English class. Nevaeh found her seat next to Rachel in the middle row and waited for Mr. Martin to start the lesson. Mr. Martin's classroom had a typical classroom look except for what he called his "Book to Movie Poster Accent Wall." The wall in the back of the classroom was filled with posters of books that were turned into movies. The wall contained a poster of "Romeo and Juliet", "The Help", "Harry Potter", "The Maze Runner", "Twilight", "Divergent", "Because of Winn Dixie", "Jurassic Park", "A Dog's Purpose", and more.

"Good morning, everyone," Mr. Martin said as he entered the room. "Please have notebooks and pens ready on your desk."

Mr. Martin was a younger teacher in his early thirties. He had dark hair and a five o'clock shadow. He always wore dress pants that were dark blue. He referred to them as his presidential pants. He always had a nice button-up shirt, and sported Texas Rangers cuff links, tie, and tie clip. He also wore glasses but took them off a lot of the time and could never remember where he put them.

"For your homework I want you to review pages twelve through fifteen in your vocabulary books. Also, please continue to work on creating hyperboles. The hyperbole assignment is due on Friday. For those of you who do not remember what a hyperbole is, it is an exaggerated statement. Make sure you write that down in your notes. For today's lesson, we will be discussing coordinating conjunctions, and reading another chapter from Harry Potter."

Mr. Martin turned and began to explain the day's lesson. "There are seven coordinating conjunctions. We can remember them by the acronym "FANBOYS". They are for, and, nor, but, or, yet, so. Any questions so far?" Mr. Martin asked.

Rachel raised her hand, and when Mr. Martin called on her, she said, "When and how would we use them?"

"I'm glad you asked" Mr. Martin responded. "Coordinating conjunctions are used to make two independent clauses and one dependent clause. For example, 'the boy went to the store. The boy bought milk while at the store.' There we have two separate independent clauses, if you will. However, if we add a coordinating conjunction to make it one dependent clause, it will flow much smoother. Watch. 'The boy went to the store and bought some milk.' Does everyone see how fluent that became?"

Coordinating conjunctions were easy to understand, but Nevaeh felt that Mr. Martin spent too much time explaining them. As the class ended, Mr. Martin asked Nevaeh to stay after class.

"I just wanted to touch base. Most of the students have turned in their ideas for their senior paper, but I haven't seen yours yet. Have you been thinking of a topic?" he asked her.

"I've been thinking about writing my paper on people with physical, or mental disabilities and how prejudices can affect their lives," she told him.

Mr. Martin smiled. "Very good. I like that idea a lot, but before I can approve that idea for you, I need to know why you chose it."

Well, ever since my accident when I lost my arm, I've had dreams of an accessible and inclusive world where people can do anything regardless of their disabilities. I want to see a world where deaf people can sing or play an instrument. They can't hear it, but they can feel the music. A world where someone with Down syndrome, or autism is allowed the same opportunities as everyone else. A world where..."

"...Individuals with one arm can play baseball?" Mr. Martin interrupted.

"Well, yeah...overall, it's a paper on why the world should be accessible and inclusive to everyone", Nevaeh said.

Mr. Martin looked at Nevaeh, wrote something on paper, and said "I'm approving your topic. I believe you are well-motivated, and I don't think you will disappoint me. I see you doing great things in your future Miss Bennet." With that, Mr. Martin dismissed her, and Nevaeh headed toward her fourth-period class.

When the school day ended, Nevaeh, Rachel, and Morgan headed to the costume store to pick out costumes for Halloween. Halloween was that weekend, and Morgan was going out trick-or-treating with her friends. Nevaeh, Rachel, and Vinny planned on giving candy out and seeing some people as well. Mrs. Bennet picked them up in her "new" van, the replacement vehicle after her husband was killed. She took them to "Colleen's Costumes". Nevaeh found a mummy costume and even found a bloody fake arm. She planned on wrapping it to her stump so it would look like her arm was barely hanging on. Rachel found a Wonder Woman costume, and Morgan found a devil costume. Vinny kept his costume a secret until Halloween night.

Halloween night was on a Saturday, so Vinny and Rachel came to Nevaeh's house early. They watched all the "scream" movies that Vinny had brought over. When it started to get dark, everyone put on their costumes. Vinny came out dressed as "Ghost Face" which explained the "scream" movies.

"You all look so cute!" Mrs. Bennet said. Everyone stood for pictures. After Mrs. Bennet's paparazzi session, Morgan left with her friends, and the other three went onto the porch to hand out candy. Overall, the night was filled with screams, laughter, friendship, and sweets.

Chapter 8

The bell rang to indicate the day's dismissal, and Nevaeh left her last-period history class.

"Where are you going?" Rachel asked. "Our lockers are this way." Nevaeh kept walking and yelled over her shoulder. "Mr. Martin wanted to see me about something and asked me to go to his classroom at the end of the day. I'll catch up."

Nevaeh knocked on Mr. Martin's classroom door and entered. "You want to see me?" she asked.

Mr. Martin was at his desk grading papers as she entered. He looked up and said, "Yes, I've been reading over your rough drafts of your senior paper, and what you have written thus far is very promising. You have remarkable ideas on inclusion for all students with disabilities. In fact, your ideas are so remarkable that I presented them to our district's athletic director, Mr. Randyll."

Nevaeh couldn't think of anything to say, so she just stared at him in disbelief. Mr. Martin continued.

"Mr. Randyll liked your ideas so much that he reached out to other districts' athletic directors. To make a long story short, all the directors were moved by your suggestions. Starting after the Thanksgiving holiday, all seven districts in the area have agreed to create special sports teams that will incorporate students with all kinds of disabilities, as well as students who do not have any disabilities. The objective is to get everyone together and have fun. Mr. Randyll also wants the coaches to be students, and he has requested you coach the specialized basketball team when we return from our Thanksgiving holiday. We know that you will be preoccupied with softball in the Spring, so we figured you could make a terrific coach for the basketball team in the interim. What do you think?"

It took Nevaeh a moment to find the words, but she finally responded. "I'm thrilled that my ideas are being taken seriously, but I don't know the first thing about basketball..."

"That's okay" Mr. Martin interrupted. "The idea is simply to include everyone and have fun. Keep in mind that this is a school function, so a teacher will be needed to supervise. I've volunteered to help, and I know a little bit about basketball. The only difference is you will be the "coach" on the sidelines, while I'm sitting in the crowd. Every district will be doing it this way and it will look good when you do your college interviews."

Nevaeh thought for a moment about this tremendous opportunity, smiled wide, and agreed. Mr. Martin was very pleased, and as he escorted Nevaeh to the door, they exchanged pleasantries for the evening.

When she met Rachel and Vinny outside, she told them the exciting news.

"I can't believe people are actually listening to my ideas!" she told them. Mrs. Bennet & Morgan were delightedly surprised at dinner that night over Nevaeh's great news! Later that night, Nevaeh tossed and turned as she tried to sleep. She kept thinking about how she was slowly making a difference. "My dad would be so proud," she thought as she finally drifted off to sleep.

The morning of Thanksgiving, Nevaeh woke to Morgan shaking her.

"Get up", Morgan said. "Mom needs our help getting the dinner ready before everyone gets here." Nevaeh sat up, rubbed her eyes, yawned, and went downstairs in her pajamas. Morgan joined Mrs. Bennet in the kitchen preparing the dishes for dinner. Sleepily, Nevaeh entered the kitchen.

"Why are you still in your pajamas?" Morgan asked. Morgan and Mrs. Bennet always woke up early to start their days, but if there was no school, Nevaeh preferred to stay up late and sleep in.

"What's wrong with my pajamas?" Nevaeh asked Morgan.

"You look like a bum!" Morgan snapped back. "Do you want Grandma and Grandpa to see you like that?"

Nevaeh shrugged. "Doesn't really matter to me," she said.

Morgan would have made another comment, but Mrs. Bennet told them to stop bickering and to behave. "It's a holiday, and I don't want to hear any more arguments," she told them. Mrs. Bennet knew only too well about the rifts between raising teenage girls. She heard many disagreements between her daughters throughout the years...and it saddened her heart...especially at holiday time when she was still mourning the tremendous loss of the love of her life. "If only Jason was here to handle their disagreements," she lamented. Yet, she knew her daughters missed their dad as well. What was there to be thankful for? "Well," she thought, "she was thankful for Jason's love and their beautiful daughters..." She was always thankful for them all.

Nevaeh went back upstairs, took a shower, dressed, and returned to the kitchen. Mrs. Bennet spent most of the morning roasting and basting the turkey and baking the apple and pumpkin pies. Morgan worked on the casseroles and Nevaeh loaded the dishwasher as dirty dishes piled in the sink.

By noon, Grandma and Grandpa arrived, inhaling the delicious aromas coming from the kitchen. Nevaeh and Morgan greeted their grandparents with hugs and kisses, and Nevaeh shared the news about the special sports teams. After all that, Grandma Bennet went to the kitchen to help cook, and Grandpa sat on the couch to watch football. Shortly after, all the girls' aunts, uncles, and cousins arrived. Soon the house sounded like a noisy mess hall waiting to be served.

When dinner was ready to eat, the family gathered around the tables. Grandma and Grandpa Bennet cut into the turkey, and the feast began. Nevaeh continued to share her story about the specialized sports teams, and Morgan began to get annoyed.

"Everything is about Nevaeh, all the time," Morgan thought to herself, but was mindful to keep quiet, especially at a holiday dinner with her Grandparents there...but it really ticked her off. "Nevaeh, Nevaeh, Nevaeh!"

The rest of the evening was filled with football, cheers, and boos, putting away the leftover food, and cleaning up the kitchen. Everyone departed by 9 p.m. and Mrs. Bennet and Morgan headed to bed. Nevaeh on the other hand, stayed awake and waited for the Black Friday shopping to begin.

At two o'clock in the morning, Nevaeh woke Morgan and her mother. They had planned to shop at the mall at 4 a.m. but Nevaeh was so bored that she woke them early. She also knew that Morgan would take forever to do her hair and makeup. By 3:30 a.m., they were in the van and on their way to the mall.

"Remember, we're all meeting back at the van by six a.m.," their mother told them, as they were getting close to the mall.

When they arrived, long lines had already formed at every store. Everyone was trying to get the best Christmas gifts at the lowest possible price. Tis the season, you know...

Nevaeh's Mom always went to the jewelry store, and the home goods store, while Morgan usually went clothes shopping. Nevaeh's goals were to stop at the video game stores, and sporting goods stores so she could find a decent gift for Vinny. Then she had to go to the nail salon for Morgan, the bookstore for Rachel, and the home goods store for her mother and grandparents. She saved the home goods store for last, hoping her mother would be done shopping there by then. Nevaeh ended up buying a gift certificate for Morgan, a book on aliens for Rachel, a Dallas Cowboys clock for her grandfather, and a new video game for Vinny. She had trouble finding gifts for her mom and grandma. She ended up buying her mom a new watch and got her grandma a new cookbook since she was always baking. By the end of the trip, Nevaeh had spent every penny she had. She had been saving her allowance, or finding odd jobs to earn the money, but it felt good buying gifts with money she earned. Nevaeh and Morgan met their mom at the van at six, as their mother requested, and they drove home, sleepy but happy with the gifts they purchased for their loved ones.

Chapter 9

As the halfway mark for the school year approached, students were preparing for their midterm exams. Nevaeh would have to take midterms in all her classes except Astronomy and History of Baseball. She would be taking final exams for those as they were only half-year courses. After the examinations were completed, the students would have a two-week holiday vacation for Christmas and New Year's. Nevaeh knew that once she returned from the holiday vacation, she would have a lot on her plate. She would need to finish, and present her Senior paper, coach the inclusive basketball team, try out for softball, and then final exams. Not to mention Prom and college visits in between everything else. Nevaeh looked forward to her upcoming challenges but put them aside to focus on her current exams. Nevaeh passed all her exams, including the exam from History of Baseball. The day before the holiday break started, Nevaeh saw Morgan during lunch and sat at her table.

"What do you want?" Morgan asked.

Nevaeh looked at Morgan with a surprised look. "Just sitting with my little sister at lunch..."

"Well, can you not? Just leave me alone," Morgan told her as she got up and walked away, angrily. Nevaeh was livid, but she let Morgan walk away.

After school, the first thing Nevaeh did was go to Morgan's room.

"What was that about today at school?"

"Oh my God!" Morgen yelled. "Just leave me alone."

"No, I will not leave you alone until you tell me what your problem with me is lately."

"I don't have a problem." Morgan lashed out at Nevaeh.

Nevaeh laughed. "Then why have you been acting weird and blowing me off since the start of the school year?"

Morgan began to cry... "You wouldn't understand", she said.

Nevaeh sat on Morgan's bed, put her arm around her, and said, "You're my sister, you can tell me anything."

Morgan let everything out. Nevaeh learned that her little sister felt jealous of her and neglected her. She told Nevaeh how she wanted to do more with her, and how it was unfair that Nevaeh had friends, a boyfriend, and was even given her own special sports team.

"It feels like nobody has time for me," she told her older sister.

By the end of their discussion, both girls were crying. Nevaeh ended up spending the night in Morgan's room watching movies and painting each other's nails.

On Christmas Eve, Nevaeh told her mom that she needed her help with a last-minute surprise for Morgan. Nevaeh handed her mom a piece of paper, and Mrs. Bennet looked uncertain.

"I don't know, Nevaeh." her mom said.

"Mom, please," Nevaeh begged. It will be good for Morgan, and I will help her if she needs it. Trust me."

Mrs. Bennet sighed. "Fine, but I better not be the one dealing with it."

Nevaeh was so excited; that she ran to the van. When she got to the van, she called Vinny and asked if they could keep Morgan's gift at his home overnight, so that they could surprise Morgan on Christmas afternoon. Vinny had planned on going to Nevaeh's around noon on Christmas, and he agreed to bring Morgan's surprise as well.

Nevaeh woke Morgan on Christmas morning by jumping on her bed at 6 a.m.!

"Get up" Nevaeh yelled. "It's Christmas!"

Nevaeh and Morgan ran downstairs and found their mother and grandparents waiting for them by the Christmas tree.

"It's about time you girls came down," their grandmother said. Morgan and Nevaeh laughed.

"What do you mean, it's six a.m.," Morgan said. Then their grandfather laughed and said, "Yes, it's early. But when you girls were younger, you would be up between four and five to see if Santa came."

"Let's open the gifts" their grandma interjected.

Soon the living room was filled with torn wrapping paper, ribbons, and bows. Morgan and Nevaeh both got clothing, nail polish, and other cosmetics from their grandparents. Their mother gave them each a set of earrings and gave Nevaeh an autographed Aaron Judge Baseball. Morgan also got an expensive, but beautiful, necklace from her mother. Morgan gave Nevaeh a new catcher's mitt with her name embroidered on it and a gift card to the movie Plex. Nevaeh gave Morgan gift certificates to the nail salon, so she and a friend could get manicures and pedicures. Morgan smiled and said, "You know I'm going to make you go with me, right?" Then both girls laughed. When they started to clean the torn wrapping paper, Nevaeh told her sister she had another surprise for her.

"What is it? WHAT IS IT?" Morgan kept asking. Finally, at noon, the doorbell rang. Morgan ran with Nevaeh to open the door. When they opened the door, Vinny was standing there with a puppy in his arms.

"Oh. My. God!! Morgan screamed, "he's so cute!!!"

"So, I take it to you like your gift?" Nevaeh asked.

"I Love, LOVE, LOVE it!!!" Morgan screamed in excitement.

"His name is Halo. That way you always have an angel, and a friend" Nevaeh told her.

Morgan put Halo down so he could roam around and gave her sister a hug, and a kiss on the cheek. After the excitement was over and Halo calmed down, Nevaeh gave Vinny his video game. Vinny pulled a small box out of his pocket and handed it to her in exchange. When Nevaeh opened her gift, she instantly began to cry. Inside the box was a locket shaped like a baseball, and inside the baseball was a picture of her and her father at Yankee Stadium.

Chapter 10

The Directors of Anthem University regularly met during the holiday vacations when the students were off campus. This year, like every other year, they converged to discuss new hires and acceptance of students. The University President Marion Fragnoli stood to announce, "We will only need to replace one of our staff members this year due to retirement." Marion Fragnoli has been the president of Anthem University for the past twelve years. She made headlines for being the first African American president at Anthem University. She was widely known and respected for her elegance, grace, and determination to education. Marion was chosen over other highly qualified candidates because of her plans to better Anthem. The last twelve years have shown higher graduation rates, as well as a large increase in applicants each year.

As Marion sat, she said, "Our head baseball coach has filed for retirement. Part of Mr. Kozlowski's contract agreement stated that he would be allowed to recommend his replacement upon the acceptance of his retirement. I am pleased to announce that the Board of Directors has accepted Mr. Kozlowski's retirement with a heavy heart. Although we are happy for the coach to begin a new chapter of his life, we are saddened to lose a wonderful man, and coach at Anthem University. With all this being said, I ask that you turn your attention towards Mr. Kozlowski as he makes a recommendation for his replacement."

Coach Kozlowski stood. "Good afternoon. I thank you for accepting my retirement. It was not an easy decision. I spent many a night debating if this would be my final season as Coach. After discussing it with my wife, we decided together that it was time to pass the torch. As many of you know, twenty years ago, our baseball team reached the National Championships, to which we lost. For forty years, I have failed. I am now a man in my seventies and have seen much in my lifetime. I have outlived some that I should not have, and even former athletes. However, for forty years I have been blind to what this team really needed. I worked diligently to be a supportive coach, but as time went on, I only wanted a championship. Many years ago, I would have said that it was my coaching that got us to the championship game. If you asked me now, I would say that it was the team that got us to the championship. Marcus Fjord was the captain of our team. It was his motivation and friendships he developed with the other players, that got the team to the championship. It was everyone's love for the sport. I used to tell them that winning or losing meant nothing, as long as they had fun and love for the sport. I told them that what defined us was how we handled defeats. As time continued, players changed, and I began to handle defeat dishonorably. I became a greedy old man who wanted nothing more than to win. A team cannot survive with a greedy coach, but a team can grow with a true leader. It is with that, and for those reasons, I have decided to retire. I believe that the right choice for the job, and for the team would be the team's former captain, Marcus Fjord."

Coach Kozlowski handed Marcus's resume to Marion. "Thank you," Marion replied. "We will look over his resume and discuss his qualifications. Marcus is in the lobby, correct?"

"That is correct, Ma'am."

"Please join him, and we will speak with you both shortly."

Coach Kozlowski and Marcus sat in the lobby as Marion and the rest of the directors discussed the request to hire Marcus as their new head coach. After thirty minutes, Marcus, and Coach Kozlowski were asked to rejoin the directors for some interview questions. Marcus and Coach Kozlowski sat in the center of a long table. Across from them sat Marion Fragnoli, and to her left and right were three directors each.

"Marcus, your accolades are well known around the university. You hold many of the University's records, and your resumé and cover letter were impressive. The directors would like to ask you a few questions." Marion told Marcus.

The directors had mostly looked pleasant except for the director on Marion's right side, George Hammerhorn. George had previously been an athletic director and took the hiring of coaches very seriously. He was muscular and short. He had dark hair, bushy dark eyebrows, and a thick dark mustache.

George looked up from his papers. "Please remind us, Mr. Fjord, why you stopped playing baseball?" he asked Marcus.

"It was a doctor's recommendation after I had Tommy John surgery," Marcus replied.

"And what have you been doing since?" George inquired.

"I have coached little league, as well as modified for elementary and middle schools," Marcus said.

"But not at a college level?" George sniggered.

"My path has not led to the collegiate level until now, sir" Marcus replied.

George made some notes on his paper and looked back at Marcus. "I will be honest, you would not be my first choice to coach this team, but my colleagues seem to think very highly of Mr. Kozlowski's decision. I, however, still struggle to accept the recommendation of a man who brought zero National Championships to the school."

"Now George," Marion interjected. "Winning championships is not what's important."

…"It most certainly IS important, Mrs. Fragnoli." George barked. "If we want this school to be everything it should be and more, we need to win championships. If I'm ever president of this

64

university, we will have qualified coaches and more championships than we could fit in this very room!"

Marion looked at George, "Well, you are not the president of this university, and I happen to value teamwork, dedication, and academics over championships." Marion proceeded to look at Marcus and said, "We voted, and decided to hire you as our head coach, Mr. Fjord. The vote was six to one, and George has made a stipulation that we re-evaluate you and your performance at the end of the season. We just need a verbal acceptance."

"I would be honored to take the position," Marcus said, as he shook Marion's hand.

"Coach Kozlowski will still coach this spring, but you can work with him, and make the needed adjustments for the transfer for the following year. Also, you will be permitted to voice opinions on the acceptance of new students who wish to play baseball." Marion told Marcus.

George coughed. "Take this for example." He slid an application and cover letter to Marcus. "She would be one of your freshmen. Take a look and tell us what you think."

Marcus read over Nevaeh Bennet's college application, cover letter, and letter of recommendation that Mr. Martin had sent in.

"It appears that Miss Bennet would be a remarkable candidate for Anthem University," replied Marcus.

"And why is that?" George asked while glaring at Marcus.

Marcus looked at George with complete certainty and said, "Well, for starters, her grades are well over average. There would be no cause for concern when it comes to her academics. From what I'm reading, she lost her arm, and her father in a tragic car accident three years ago, yet she is still determined and completes every goal she sets for herself. That's very admirable, especially after such an enormous loss as hers. The letter from her English teacher states that she has worked hard to create an environment that is inclusive and accessible to mentally, and physically disabled individuals. Everything that I'm seeing indicates that she would be an exemplary student here at Anthem."

"And to what do you make of her goals with baseball?" George asked.

"I see no harm in meeting with the young lady and allowing her an opportunity..." Marcus said.

..."You would rather see a cripple on our baseball team, and a girl nonetheless?" George interrupted.

Marcus kept his patience. "I would see no harm in allowing an opp..."

"So, we're going to a team full of cripples? How can we expect to win a championship if you're going to allow every Joe Shmo to play on the team?" George yelled.

Marcus remained calm. "If you would allow me to finish. I see no harm in allowing an opportunity. She may very well be one of the best players to ever step foot on a baseball diamond. And I believe in giving people a chance."

George laughed. "A cripple will be no good on the diamond. You should know that yourself. You also seem to forget that she is a girl!"

"She is trying to create an inclusive and accessible world!" Marcus said losing his patience. "There is no better way to increase Anthem University's interest than by allowing opportunities that others won't allow. Gender and disabilities don't define people. It would do you good, Mr. Hammerhorn, to learn that."

"Don't you tell me what I should and shouldn't learn, boy", George yelled at Marcus.

Marcus refused to yell. "From what I can see, this '*girl*' is probably the very person this university needs. She can probably teach us all something!"

The way that Marcus spoke only seemed to enrage George even more. "This girl, and a cripple at that, will not bring us a championship. I am sick and tired of seeing this university lose. I refuse to allow this school to be defined as a failure, and home to a crippled sports team," George Hammerhorn angrily exclaimed!

The rest of the meeting members watched intently as this meeting became like a tennis match between players. But Marcus was holding his own against George Hammerhorn, and this was definitely a plus for all those who voted for Marcus. It was 15 – love, to say the least.

Marcus smiled. "Well, sir. It seems that I have been chosen as the new baseball coach, not you, Mr. Hammerhorn. If Mrs. Fragnoli decides to accept Nevaeh Bennet into Anthem University after my recommendation, then I will afford her a fair and equal opportunity to play baseball."

George continued to yell..." then the university better prepare for yet another loss." George looked at Marion and the other directors and emphatically said, "I hope you're happy with your decision! We've already lost!"

Marcus Fjord stood from his seat. "Mr. Hammerhorn, you're acknowledging the loss of a championship that has yet to happen. The only loss that I can see that you have suffered here was your campaign to hire someone other than me. A wise man once told me that what defines us is how we handle defeat. And, well, sir...I think we have all learned quite a bit about you this evening, Mr. Hammerhorn."

Thirty - love. Or better yet, in Marcus Fjord's world...Homerun!

Chapter 11

True to her word, Morgan made Nevaeh go to the nail salon with her to get a manicure and pedicure...a mani/pedi as commonly known among the teens. Nevaeh chose to go with a dark cobalt blue on her fingers and toes. Morgan chose pink for their fingers and purple for their toes. Vinny had volunteered to play with Halo at the park in order to allow the two sisters some "girl time". Once the girls were finished, they went to the food court at the mall to grab a bite to eat.

"Make sure you eat up," Nevaeh told Morgan. "I have one more surprise before we go home."

"What is it?" Morgan asked, curiosity building.

"Well, since you used your gift certificate on us, I decided to use mine on us, too. We're going to go see that movie you wanted to see."

"The one about the boy and girl falling in love?" Morgan asked excitedly. Nevaeh laughed. "That's the one, and the best part is Vinny is going to pick us up and drop Halo off at home. I told him we were going to watch that new action movie. I can't wait to see the look on his face." Both girls started to laugh!

"I guess that movie wasn't too bad," Vinny told Nevaeh on their way home.

"So that means you'll watch more romance movies with me?" Nevaeh asked laughing.

After Vinny dropped them off at home, Nevaeh knew she should work on her Senior paper. It was only Friday night, but the deadline was fast approaching. And she didn't want to leave it to the last minute. There was much to be conveyed in her Senior paper, and that had to be said in her research. She wanted to get it all written down, perfectly. This would count towards getting into an amazing college, and that's what she intended to do, no holds barred. So, an evening of fun with her sister Morgan, and boyfriend, Vinny, meant a weekend of research and writing her term paper. She was committed to the effort. Nevaeh worked diligently until Rachel called her later that evening. She spent the rest of the night talking to Rachel about Vinny, and the girls spent a lot of time giggling, as girls with boyfriends do. Nevaeh was truly a procrastinator and found a ton of excuses to blow off her paper over the weekend, disregarding her commitment to the research and Senior paper. She didn't realize there would be so many distractions. When Sunday night rolled around, she found herself sitting at her desk, using her "speech-to-text converter" well into the night, much to her dismay, and against her principles. "Well," she thought to herself, "tomorrow is another day" ... but another day closer to the term paper's deadline and needing to be turned in...

One of the requirements for the Senior Paper was to create a slideshow presentation. The paper itself was turned in to Mr.

Martin, but they still had to present their topic to the class. The presentations happened in alphabetical order by last name. That meant that Nevaeh had to go second behind Ashley Adams. Ashley gave her presentation on the effects of smoking tobacco and made an argument that tobacco should be illegal. When it was Nevaeh's turn to present, she said, "Like Martin Luther King Jr. had a dream in the past, I have a dream today." Nevaeh proceeded to explain how she dreamed of a world that was inclusive, and accessible in every aspect for people with disabilities. She detailed how jobs, sports, colleges, and more are needed to create fair and equal opportunities for all individuals. Nevaeh pointed out how individuals with Autism, Down's syndrome, or other forms of mental disabilities were not given the same opportunities as others. She showed examples of people being denied jobs due to physical disabilities such as only having one arm. "Of course, employees will make up a different reason you didn't get the job," she told the class. By the end of her presentation, everyone sat in silence.

"That's not fair that people are treated that way," a boy in the back of the class said. Mr. Martin stood and said, "precisely Nevaeh's point. She did an excellent job showing the unjustified cruelty to people with disabilities. Everyone, please gift her with a round of applause." And everyone stood, and gave Nevaeh a resounding standing ovation, with cheers of praise intermittently. Nevaeh was so proud, that she couldn't contain her tears, which flowed freely. Everyone in the classroom continued to applaud as Nevaeh found her seat.

When Nevaeh and Morgan got off the bus, Morgan checked the mailbox, and Nevaeh headed inside. Nevaeh was relieved that her Senior Presentation was completed and planned on watching the television for the rest of the afternoon.

"You have mail," Morgan said as she threw four envelopes on Nevaeh's lap. Nevaeh noticed that the return address on each envelope was different. She had a letter from Texas Community College, Anthem University, Paramount University, and Elementz State College.

"These must be my acceptance or rejection letters." Nevaeh thought. She had butterflies in the pit of her stomach as she started to open the letters. Nevaeh began with the letter from "TCC" and was offered admission.

"They accept everyone." Nevaeh thought. She opened Paramount University's letter next.

"Dear Miss Bennet,

We thank you for applying for admission to Paramount University. We regret to inform you that our Physical Therapy and Sports Management Program are currently full; and as a result, must deny your request for admission. We have reviewed your academic records and believe that you would be a terrific addition to our

program, but our space is limited. However, we will keep
your application on file and encourage you to apply again
next semester.

Best Wishes,

Tyler M. Jacobs

Paramount University President"

"Damn it!" Nevaeh said after reading the letter from Paramount.

Morgan looked away from the television. "What?" she asked Nevaeh. "I got accepted to TCC, but Paramount denied me," Nevaeh said disbelievingly.

"Why?" Morgan asked.

"Not enough space, I guess. And then, nothing about baseball in either," Nevaeh answered.

"Well, you still have two letters to open," Morgan said. Nevaeh chose to open Elementz State College next.

"Dear Miss Bennet,

After careful consideration of your academics, character letters, and sports history, Elementz State College of New York is honored to offer you admission into our coveted physical therapy and sports management program. As you are well aware, our program has led to success for our students. As I am sure you are also aware, Elementz State College is the proud champion of the last seven national championships for baseball and has obtained eleven softball national championships (though not consecutively). Students enter our sports teams as freshmen and leave with multiple championships as graduating seniors. I have personally spoken with our head softball coach, Lisa Juber, and would like to invite you to our softball tryouts. I have enclosed Ms. Juber's email and number as well as my own. Please carefully consider our offer of acceptance and let us know prior to May 17th.

Yours truly,

C. J. Snow

ESC   NY President"

Nevaeh finished reading and looked at Morgan.

"Well?" Morgan asked.

"I got accepted, but they only mention softball," Nevaeh told her. Morgan tried to be happy but said, "New York City is really far away anyway. Plus, you still have a letter from Anthem. She scratched Halo behind the ears. "I really hope you get accepted into Anthem. I don't want to lose my sister, at least at Anthem, you would be close. TCC, too. Morgan said.

"Looks like I'll be stuck going to TCC," Nevaeh thought. "I have a bad feeling about Anthem," Nevaeh told Morgan.

"Just open it," Morgan told her.

When Nevaeh opened the envelope, she found two letters, instead of one. The first one read,

"Dear Miss Bennet,

Each year the directors of Anthem University meet with me to discuss upcoming changes for our academic years. One of the changes we discussed is the students that we would like to accept into our university. Each of our directors has reviewed your application, cover letter, and reference letters. To say that we are pleased would be an understatement. Your academics remain above average, and you have assisted your community in many ways. With that being said, it is a pleasure to offer you acceptance to Anthem University, and the Sports Management Program.

Anthem University strives to be different than our neighboring universities. Anthem believes in giving everyone a fair opportunity. Anthem gave me an opportunity when they elected to hire me as their President. Being a female of color, I was overlooked for many jobs similar. We have hired a new baseball coach as well and given him an opportunity to win a championship that he came very close to in his youth. Mr. Fjord and I would not only like to offer you acceptance to the University, but we would like to "pay it forward" and offer you a fair and equal opportunity to play on our baseball team. Enclosed you will find a letter from Mr. Fjord, as well as our contact information. Please reach out to us if you have any questions. Lastly, we will be doing campus visits in two months' time. I ask that you visit the university and speak with Mr. Fjord and me before making any decisions. I will look forward to your call or email to set up a visitation.

Grace & Peace,

Marion Fragnoli

Anthem University President"

"I don't believe it!" Nevaeh shrieked with excitement.

"What!? What does it say?" Morgan asked.

"I got accepted" Nevaeh paused and smiled. "And they're going to let me try out for their baseball team!"

Morgan got excited! "You're sure it says baseball and not soft..."

"B.A.S.E" Nevaeh spelled out. "Clear as day, and there's a letter from the new coach."

"Read it out loud," Morgan asked, "Please!!"

Nevaeh opened his letter and began to read.

"Dear Miss Bennet,

If you accept, your freshman year will also be my first year coaching at the collegiate level. After reading your cover letter and references, I can't imagine a better fit at Anthem University. Although we have never won a championship, the team at Anthem is where you would want to be. Our baseball team will pride ourselves on, in your words, being "accessible and inclusive" for all. Our team will be more than a team. We will be a family. We will teach others that championships do not define a team.

I am not great at writing letters, so I hope you accept this brief note, and join us for visitation to see if Anthem University would be a good fit for you. Also, please keep in mind that this is an invitation for you to a fair opportunity. It does not necessarily mean that you will

make the team. Practice hard, stay safe, and hopefully, I
will see you on the Diamond soon.

Sincerely,

Marcus Fjord

Anthem University Head Baseball Coach"

"At least he is going to give you an opportunity," Morgan said.

Nevaeh hugged her sister and screamed with excitement. Halo ran off at Nevaeh's scream.

Nevaeh and Morgan were still screaming with excitement when their mother came home from work.

"What is with all the screaming?" Mrs. Bennet asked. "I thought someone was hurt!"

Nevaeh handed the letters from Marion Fragnoli, and Marcus Fjord to her mother. Once Mrs. Bennet finished reading, she quickly joined the girls in their screaming. By then, Halo was so excited, that he began to howl as well. Nevaeh called all her grandparents, and as all grandparents are, they were so very proud of their granddaughter! Her Aunts, Uncles, and cousins would find out soon, through the family grapevine... Nevaeh couldn't help but think..." if only Dad could see me..." But she knew only too well, that he would be so proud of her, and he was always looking out for her, and Morgan, too. After all, they were his baby girls.

Chapter 12

After Nevaeh shared the news of Anthem's acceptance with everyone, she spent most of her time in the backyard practicing with Vinny or coaching the all-inclusive basketball team. The first day with the basketball team was very stressful for Nevaeh. She spent most of the day trying to learn plays and was nervous she would blow it. Once she gathered with all the students, she realized that most of them didn't care about winning, they were just glad to have an opportunity to play and have fun. Nevaeh continued to work with the basketball team. In fact, playing basketball and helping others feel important became one of her favorite pastimes. Nevaeh's heart was filled with joy. Vinny, Morgan, and Rachel were on the basketball team as well; and Nevaeh loved seeing them all interact with the other students. The basketball team was such a huge success that the local newspaper did an article when Mr. Martin and Nevaeh were interviewed. Mr. Martin was quoted saying "Nevaeh Bennet developed plans to start a sports team that contained all students, and students with disabilities, or rather, different abilities. She then worked hard to make that dream a reality. She's a pioneer and is going to achieve greatness." Most of the article praised Nevaeh, except for her own quotation. "I don't want fame or credit. All that's important to me is that this team has brought people together who normally wouldn't gather. This team has given everyone a fair chance to play and brought happiness along the way. I couldn't ask for more."

One day at one of the basketball games, the team was warming up when Rebecca came up to Nevaeh and told her that something happened to Vinny, and she needed to go out to the hallway as soon as possible. Rebecca was a girl on Nevaeh's team who had Down syndrome.

"What happened to him?" Nevaeh asked, nervously.

"Just come with me," Rebecca said as she grabbed Nevaeh's wrist and dragged her to the hallway.

When Nevaeh reached the hallway, she couldn't believe her eyes. The hall was filled with colorful balloons and streamers. Above the entrance to the next hall, a banner hung that read, "PROM?", and underneath the banner, Vinny stood with a bouquet of flowers waiting for an answer. Nevaeh was stunned! "H-H-How..." was all she could get out. Mr. Martin helped me get use of the hallway," Vinny told her. Nevaeh still shocked, asked, "How long have you been planning this?" "Oh, since about October," Vinny said with a big smile on his face. "And I'm not good at keeping secrets so this is an accomplishment for me," he laughed.

Nevaeh said nothing, and hugged him, with a gentle little kiss on his cheek.

"So, does this mean you'll go with me?" he asked.

"Of course, I'll go with you, doofus!" she said with tears stinging her eyes. "You're so sweet!" As they walked back into the gymnasium, they heard pop, pop, pop, and confetti started to fall all around them. The entire team was shooting confetti poppers. Nevaeh looked at Vinny and said, "I think you overdid this 'promposal.'" Vinny laughed and said, "Hey! The confetti was Rachel's idea."

The following weekend, Nevaeh and Rachel went shopping for Prom dresses. Rachel had been asked to the Prom by Keven. Keven was a deaf boy who played on the basketball team. Rachel thought he was cute, so she started taking sign language classes shortly after the team developed. Rachel was head over heels with the fact that Keven asked her to prom, and even tried to teach Nevaeh some sign language so that she could talk to Keven too.

"I'm not very good at this sign language with only having one arm," Nevaeh thought. "And Rachel isn't either with two arms. It's a good thing Keven can read lips and speak well."

"I don't know who's more excited for prom," Nevaeh told Rachel as she was driving them to "Luxury Dresses and Tuxedos" at the mall.

"What do you mean?" Rachel asked.

"Nothing," Nevaeh laughed. "You have just been acting crazy ever since Keven asked.

Rachel laughed. "I know I've been a little overboard. It's just a guy finally noticed me."

"I guess that's a good enough reason to be super giddy," Nevaeh said. When they pulled into the parking lot at the mall, they could barely find a place to park. Eventually, they found an open spot at the far end of the lot.

"I hope we don't run into anyone from school," Rachel said.

"I don't care who we see. I just hope no one buys the same dress as me," Nevaeh laughed.

"Do you know what color dress you want?" Rachel asked Nevaeh.

"Red! How about you?" Nevaeh asked Rachel.

"I should have known you would pick your favorite color. Color doesn't matter to me. I just want something pretty," Rachel. "It's such a beautiful occasion, and I want to look my best...for Keven."

Shopping for a prom dress took a lot longer than they thought it would. Not only was the store crowded, but each girl tried on twenty or more dresses. It was exhausting! But eventually, both girls fell in love with a dress. Nevaeh found a long red dress that only hung over her left shoulder. "Perfect for my one-arm self," she thought. The dress had a leg slit to make walking easier and had beautiful gathers in all the right places. It was stunning on her. Rachel found a long strapless dress. It was lavender in color and covered in shiny sequins. When the girls left the Luxury Dresses and Tuxedos shop, they had both spent over $200 on a dress, and it was dark outside.

"Wow!" Rachel exclaimed. "We were in there for hours!"

"Too long," Nevaeh said, "I'm tired!"

Rachel stayed the night at Nevaeh's and both girls found a pair of heels online to match their dresses. All they had to do now was wait until prom night...but they had to remember to order boutonnieres for Vinny and Keven, as well.

Prom was still three weeks away and Nevaeh put prom behind her so she could focus on softball tryouts. "I'm ready to prove I can play," she thought.

"What position are you trying out for?" Coach Fisher asked Nevaeh.

"Catcher" she replied.

Coach Fisher looked uneasy at Nevaeh, but put her behind the plate, regardless. Coach Fisher had Erin Munnings pitch to her. Erin was a Senior, and the best pitcher on the softball team. At first, Nevaeh stumbled. She had been used to Vinny throwing pitches to her overhand and off a mound. In softball, they threw on flat dirt, and underhand. Nevaeh quickly readjusted and was blocking and catching every pitch.

"Let's see your snap throws to second" Coach Fisher yelled out.

Every pitch that came at Nevaeh she caught. It didn't matter if it was a fastball or a curveball. If it was thrown, it ended in Nevaeh's glove. Nevaeh showed how she mastered catching the ball, tossing it into the air, dropping the glove, re-grabbing the ball, and throwing it to second.

"Impressive!" Coach Fisher said. "And that's your nondominant hand?"

"That's right!" Nevaeh said happily. She felt very proud about how tryouts went. As Nevaeh was taking off the catcher's gear in the locker room, she had trouble unstrapping the breastplate.

"Do you need help?" Coach Fisher asked.

"Please," Nevaeh responded. "It's hard reaching around with one arm to undo the strap.

Coach Fisher helped her out and said, "That was really impressive out there."

"Thank you! Do you know when you will have the list posted?" Nevaeh asked.

"The list of names will be posted the Monday after prom; I want to make sure any players I choose can manage to behave at prom. There's no better way to enforce proper behavior by leaving them in suspense." Coach Fisher laughed as Nevaeh was leaving the locker room, saying "Nice to see you today, Coach". He acknowledged her departure..." you too, Nevaeh."

Nevaeh thought to herself, "Make sure I follow every rule at Prom" as she left the locker room. "I can't miss this opportunity!"

After all the excitement of prom dress shopping, and softball tryouts, the following week was quiet. Her Mom, Mrs. Bennet loved both Nevaeh's and Rachel's dresses...she knew it would be a beautiful evening for both girls. Morgan couldn't wait until her prom, and she'd be dressed to the hilt with all her hair and nail and beauty techniques! She'd be the prettiest one there at her prom!

The basketball season was coming to an end, and prom was the upcoming weekend. All Nevaeh had to do was get through the week, and prom would be waiting. The week dragged by, not only for Nevaeh, but for Vinny, Keven, and Rachel as well. They were all excited for the Senior Prom, and it seemed like it would never come.

When Saturday finally got here, everyone met at Nevaeh's house before the prom. Vinny and Keven paid for a limo to take them to and from prom, but the limo was still an hour away from arriving. Mrs. Bennet wanted pictures as she wanted memories of every major event. Morgan had volunteered to be the photographer due to her photography class she took as an elective. After pictures of them exchanging boutonnières and wrist corsages, and an hour of Morgan barking commands and poses, the limousine arrived. Morgan continued to snap photographs of the four teens getting into the limo and driving away. "It's good to have candid pictures," she told her mother.

The school district rented the local nightclub for the location of the prom. When the limo arrived, everyone was in awe. The building was huge, and they could only imagine what the inside looked like. The district had set the outside to look like a "red carpet" event. In fact, there was even a red carpet, lights, and other decorations that made the students feel as if they were rich and famous as they entered the nightclub. When they entered the building, their mouths hit the floor! There were numerous tables for eating and resting, a buffet to the side with an ice sculpture of their school mascot, a dolphin, and many different drinks. In the center of the room was a large dance floor. The lights were dim, and when the DJ played music, neon lights flashed throughout the dance floor and broke into several gorgeous beams once they hit the chandelier.

"It's so beautiful!" Rachel said and sighed. They all agreed. It was truly something to behold, a memory that would last forever!

After they ate, the rest of the night consisted of dancing, chatting with their classmates, and laughing. Cameras were taking pictures of couples with different settings. Everyone was enjoying themselves. When the last slow song played, Nevaeh and Vinny danced. Nevaeh thought the night was over, but suddenly the emcee called that it was time to announce the Prom King and Queen.

Nevaeh completely forgot about Prom King and Queen. They all cast their votes anonymously when they entered but thought nothing of it since whoever the winners were had to dance together in front of everyone to a slow song. In past years, the announcement of a king and queen has ruined relationships and caused fights. The winners were chosen by the male who had the most votes, and the female who had the most votes. Not the couple.

"I hope Rachel gets Prom Queen," Nevaeh thought. "Vinny has always been popular enough to win king, I just hope my best friend gets it too." Nevaeh crossed her fingers and waited for the announcement.

"Alright, Alright, Alright!" The emcee announced. "It's time to crown your king and queen."

Everyone grew silent and gave full attention to the DJ. "Ladies and Gentlemen" The DJ's voice grew deep. "Your King has been chosen...drum roll, please...And the King is...VINCENT GREEN!"

Vinny stood, giving Nevaeh a soft kiss on her cheek, and walked to the front of the crowd. The DJ placed the crown on top of Vinny's head, and Vinny awaited his Queen.

"Your Queen has been chosen!" the DJ announced in the same deep voice as before. The DJ showed Vinny the card that pronounced his Queen, and Vinny whispered something in his ear. "According to your King, your chosen Queen is one of the most outgoing, and beautiful people his grace has ever met," the DJ declared.

Everyone stood watching as the DJ said, "Drum roll, please...And your Prom Queen is...according to your King, the most talented catcher to ever step foot behind the plate...and his girlfriend...NEVAEH BENNET!!"

Nevaeh felt a pit in her stomach as everyone cheered! She never expected to win Prom Queen. She walked to the front of the crowd, and stood next to Vinny, exchanging grins and hugs with Vinny. The DJ placed the crown on her head as the photographer took pictures. "It's time for the King and Queen to lead us in our final dance," the DJ announced. Nevaeh and Vinny went to the center of the dance floor and began to dance to the music. Halfway through the dance, Nevaeh rested her head on Vinny's chest and thought, "This night is perfect. I don't ever want it to end."

Chapter 13

The following Monday, the students returned to school, and everyone took to calling Nevaeh and Vinny "Your Grace" after the DJ had referred to them as such. When the bell rang indicating the end of the school day, Nevaeh grabbed Rachel and headed towards the Gymnasium to check the softball list. Vinny went with them as well. He didn't need to check the baseball list since he had been the starting catcher for the last three years, but he wanted to lend his support to Nevaeh. When they reached the bulletin board outside of the Gym, Nevaeh ran her fingers down the list and found her name. Below the list of names is the date and time of their first practice.

"Shoot!" Nevaeh said.

"What?" Vinny and Rachel both asked at the exact same time.

"You made the team, right?" Vinny followed up.

Yeah, I made the team, but the first practice is scheduled for the same time I'm supposed to visit Anthem," Nevaeh said. "I'm going to email Mrs. Fragnoli to see if I can reschedule the visit."

To Nevaeh's delight, Marion Fragnoli agreed to reschedule for the following day.

On Saturday, Nevaeh grabbed all her catcher's gear, and the glove that Morgan got her for Christmas, and left for practice. When Nevaeh arrived at the field, Erin was already practicing her pitching. Nevaeh walked up to Shelby and said, "Excuse me", so that Nevaeh could catch Erin's pitches. Shelby was the team's other catcher and served as a backup catcher for the last two years.

"Why would I move?" Shelby snapped. Nevaeh was taken aback. "I just figured..."

"That you would catch for me?" Erin interjected. "Maybe you should talk to Coach Fisher." Shelby got up, covered her mouth with her glove, and whispered something to Erin. Both girls started to laugh as they walked away. "What was that all about?" Nevaeh thought.

"Coach Fisher!" Nevaeh yelled as she ran to her coach. "Erin said that you wanted to talk to me?"

Coach Fisher looked Nevaeh up and down. "It's good to see that you made it, but you won't be needing all that equipment on the bench."

"The bench?" Nevaeh asked, confused.

"Yes, the bench," Coach Fisher said rudely. "You know, the long wooden thing that the backups sit on."

"Back up?" Nevaeh asked...

Coach Fisher grunted. "I don't know how much more clearly I can make this, Nevaeh." He began to speak slower. "You...will...sit...on...the...bench. You're the backup catcher."

"Wait" Nevaeh blurted out. "Why am I the backup? You, yourself said that I was impressive the other day."

"Yes, you were impressive," Coach Fisher said sharply. "Everything was impressive until I realized you were unable to unstrap your breastplate by yourself. It made me wonder what other simple tasks you would fail at, and personally, I want to win games, not lose them."

Nevaeh stood there frozen. "I don't even know what to say," she thought.

"Well, don't just stand there" Fisher yelled. "There's a bench that needs warming."

"Coach Fisher," Nevaeh began. "I disagree with your opinion. I think I'm very skilled behind..."

"Yes, yes." Fisher interrupted, waving his hand. "Everyone thinks very highly of themselves. If truth be told, Erin and some of the other girls don't feel comfortable playing with someone who has...a condition, such as yours."

"A condition?" Nevaeh said incredulously. "That's not even fair! I didn't ask to lose my arm, or my father in an accident."

"Oh, Miss Bennet, the pity card won't work here. If you don't like my decision, you can always leave the team. You should be grateful I even awarded you an opportunity." Fisher responded.

Nevaeh didn't miss a beat. "I don't want to play on a team where people look down on others. Find yourself a new backup." With that, Nevaeh left the field while the other girls laughed. When Nevaeh got home, she ran past Morgan, went to her room, and cried. Morgan and Halo followed.

"What's wrong?" Morgan asked.

Nevaeh was too upset to answer. Halo cocked his head and licked Nevaeh's cheek. Nevaeh eventually stopped crying and told Morgan what had happened at the softball field. Nevaeh stayed in her room for the rest of the night, but Morgan left Halo so she wouldn't be alone. When Mrs. Bennet returned home, Morgan explained why Nevaeh was in her room, and Mrs. Bennet, Morgan, and Nevaeh headed to Anthem University for the visit.

When they arrived, Nevaeh was stunned by how beautiful the campus was. Anthem University sat on a lake and made the view breathtaking from any window. The school mascot was a wolf, and there was a water fountain in front of the main doors. The fountain consisted of three wolves howling, while the water shot out of their mouths into the center. As many potential students were visiting, the University hung several banners encouraging them to join "The Wolfpack." Nevaeh arrived early for her visitation, but Marion Fragnoli was ready. "You must be Miss. Bennet." Mrs. Fragnoli said as Nevaeh walked in. Nevaeh shook her hand and said, "Mrs. Fragnoli, it's a pleasure to meet you." Before Nevaeh could meet Marcus, they had to complete a tour of the facility. There were five different buildings where classes would be held. Each building was dedicated to its respective category. There was a building dedicated to English, Math, History, and Science. The fifth building was dedicated to physical Education, art, music, and other half-year electives. Nevaeh would be spending most of her time in the science and elective building since her major was Physical Therapy and Sports Management. Nevaeh was already in love with the college, and the dorms were beautiful. She could only imagine what their sports fields looked like.

When Mrs. Fragnoli took Nevaeh and her family to the baseball diamond, Nevaeh was not disappointed. The field was taken care of very well, and the atmosphere made her feel at home.

"Nevaeh, I would like to introduce you to Coach Kozlowski, and Coach Fjord," Mrs. Fragnoli said.

"It's a pleasure to meet you both," Nevaeh said. As Nevaeh shook Marcus's hand, she thought he looked familiar, but she was unable to place from when or where she knew him.

Coach Kozlowski approached. "I know that you will be trying out when Marcus is Coach, but what do you say you let me see your skills behind the plate as well?" he asked.

"Sure!" Nevaeh replied enthusiastically. "I didn't bring my glove though."

"That's okay," Coach Kozlowski said, "we keep spare equipment in the shed."

Marcus ran to the shed and grabbed a glove and some gear for Nevaeh. The baseball team had gathered for practice, so Nevaeh would be facing real batters and real runners.

"This is an early chance to prove myself," Nevaeh thought as Marcus handed her the equipment.

"Kyle Swabell will pitch to you," Coach Kozlowski told Nevaeh. "If you make the team when Mr. Fjord is coach, Kyle will be a senior and our ace. Best if you get used to his pitches now."

Nevaeh went out onto the field and played everything perfectly. She caught all of Kyle's pitches, blocked his pitches in the dirt, and threw out their best runner at second. As the two coaches watched, they had a small conversation.

"By the looks of her, you would be a fool to cut her," Kozlowski told Marcus.

"I'm well aware. Did you notice how she mustered that catch and grab?" "I did, and I hear it's her non-dominant hand," Kozlowski stated.

"That makes it all the more impressive," Marcus said. "She might even be better than her dad."

"When do you plan on telling her that you used to pitch to her father?" Kozlowski asked.

"Not just yet. We need to give it time, and let her find her own place first," Marcus replied.

"I see, and I agree," Kozlowski said. "Well, this isn't a tryout. We better call her in."

When Nevaeh came back to the dugouts, both coaches told her how impressed they were. "I fully expect to see you at tryouts next year," Marcus told her. "Are you playing softball in High School currently?"

Nevaeh explained the story of what happened the day before with Coach Fisher and the other girls. When she was finished explaining, Coach Kozlowski made an offer.

"How would you feel about assisting the team this year? Kind of like an apprentice?"

Nevaeh could not contain her excitement. "I would love to!" she said. Another golden opportunity!

Chapter 14

As May approached, Nevaeh's life began to turn hectic once more. She found that her schedule always seemed packed, and she had to add final exams and graduation to her very growing list of things to accomplish. On top of assisting Anthem's Baseball team, her approaching eighteenth birthday, and academics, her mom dropped another bombshell.

"I scheduled a road test for you on May 22nd. I think it's past time that you've gotten your license to drive.

"Okay!" Nevaeh answered excitedly. That's two days before my birthday, so if I pass, can I borrow the van?" she asked laughing.

"We'll see," her mother replied.

Later that night, Nevaeh assisted the coaches at one of the baseball games. Once Nevaeh officially accepted her admission to Anthem, Coach Kozlowski gave her a black t-shirt that had "Anthem" in bright gold letters across the chest to wear while she was helping. Nevaeh usually handed bats to players and gathered balls for the umpire. Essentially, she was Anthem's bat girl. She also learned a lot from listening to the two coaches talk. The only thing that Nevaeh didn't like was her T-shirt. She wanted a uniform like everyone else. The uniforms consisted of half-black and half-red tops that split diagonally. One sleeve was red, while the other was black. The diagonal line that separated the two colors was a light blue baseball seam that included stitches and all. Across the chest in bright gold letters read "Anthem," and on the back of the jerseys were the player's name and number, also in gold. The rest of the uniform consisted of dark grey bottoms, black cleats, and a red hat with a golden A.

"Soon enough I will make the team and get my own uniform," Nevaeh would tell herself.

If Nevaeh wasn't with the baseball team, or studying for her final exams, she could most likely be found in the backyard practicing with Vinny or practicing her parallel parking for her road test. Soon, her final exams started, and May 22nd approached.

"Are you excited to get your license?" Morgan asked as their mother drove them to the DMV.

"Nervous" Nevaeh answered.

Morgan laughed. "Don't be. You'll do fine."

Soon, Morgan and Mrs. Bennet were sitting inside of the DMV waiting eagerly to hear the results of Nevaeh's road test. When Nevaeh walked in with her head down, Morgan immediately thought she failed.

"Well...?" Morgan asked.

Nevaeh feigned sorrow. "Well...I PASSED!!" she yelled. After getting all the official paperwork signed and paid for,

Nevaeh drove home that afternoon, and Mrs. Bennet allowed her to take the van to Anthem's game that night.

Two days later on the morning of Nevaeh's eighteenth birthday, Morgan woke her at 9:00 a.m.

"Come downstairs!" Morgan yelled, "Mom has a surprise for you."

Morgan ran out of the room before Nevaeh could respond. Nevaeh sat up, slid her feet into her New York Yankees slippers, and proceeded to go downstairs in her pajamas.

"Morgan and I only got you one gift this year," her mother said as she handed Nevaeh a small box. Nevaeh took the box and opened it only to find a key.

"A key?" Nevaeh asked.

"Look in the driveway, fool," Morgan said.

Nevaeh walked to the window, pushed the curtain aside, and couldn't believe her eyes. In the driveway, a brand-new Chevy Equinox sat with a giant red bow on top.

"Your dad always meant to buy you a car when you turned sixteen. I had to push it back a few years, but it's finally here," her mother said. Nevaeh hugged her mom. "I love it! Thank you so so so much!" she cried. Nevaeh quickly showered, dressed, and called Rachel and Vinny. Shortly after, she was driving off in her new Equinox to show her friends.

Soon after Nevaeh's birthday, there were final exams, and the school year came to an end. She passed all her exams and received her cap and gown. All Nevaeh had to do now was wait for graduation night and she would be one step closer to moving into Anthem and playing baseball. The last final exam was on May 28th, which meant that graduation fell on the following Friday, June 4th. It felt like a fortnight, and Nevaeh thought that graduation would never come. Eventually, June 3rd came, and Nevaeh joined her classmates for a rehearsal of the graduation ceremony. Rachel was the Class Valedictorian, and Alyssa Moonstone was the salutatorian. Nevaeh asked Rachel about her speech, but Rachel said she was keeping that a secret until the following night.

On Friday, many families gathered inside the school's auditorium to watch as the students crossed the stage to get their diplomas. After everyone got their diplomas, Rachel made her speech.

"Although each and every one of us will go our separate ways, we have all interacted with each other one way or another. Many years ago, we came into school, and sat as strangers, not knowing what to expect. Today, we rise, not only as graduates but as friends and families. We live in a world that sees too much prejudice. We live in a world that doesn't offer equal opportunities. I have been honored to be a part of this school and of this class. I have watched us all make changes to better the world. My best friend was a part of that. Although this speech is short, this message will still be spread through my fellow classmates. The students you see behind me will make the world a better place, and more inclusive. As my best friend, Nevaeh Bennet said during her Senior Presentation, 'Martin Luther King, Jr. once had a dream and I do, too'. We all dream of a more inclusive world, and because we were all here, we'll make that possible. We sat together as strangers four years ago, but we rise united. As one, I will forever be thankful to be a Dolphin."

As Rachel finished her speech, everyone stood and applauded. The speech brought tears to Nevaeh, and there really wasn't a dry eye in the auditorium. Nevaeh had not expected Rachel to deliver such a beautiful speech. "She was always so timid," she thought. When graduation was over, the school principal announced that they had one final award to give out.

"As many of you know, four years ago, we lost a former student to a terrible accident. At that time, our staff decided to memorialize Jason Bennet, but we needed to wait until the right moment."

Nevaeh, Morgan, their Grandparents, and Mrs. Bennet all began to cry. The principal continued.

"Jason Bennet was a respectful, kind, outgoing, and overall friendly man. Jason would have given the shirt off his back to anyone in need. Jason would not tolerate bullying and included everyone in activities. This award is to be presented to the graduating senior who exhibits those qualities. This year's recipient and the first winner of the Annual Jason Bennet Memorial Award has exhibited the previously mentioned qualities to a high degree. It is only fitting that the recipient of the $10,000 scholarship, and Jason Bennet Memorial Award be awarded to his daughter...Nevaeh Bennet."

As everyone applauded, Nevaeh stood with tears streaming down her face to accept her award. Nevaeh gave a small thank-you speech and posed for a photograph. "I hope they don't see my tears," she thought. "They were tears of joy though."

After the ceremony, the graduates and families gathered in the cafeteria for a delicious luncheon...their last time together as a class... Many people congratulated Nevaeh on her award, and Rachel on her wonderful speech. When everyone began to leave, Nevaeh looked at Vinny Rachel and Keven.

It's officially summer, and we're college-bound," she said, partly sad and partly ecstatic.

As summer began, Nevaeh found that she had more free time than she originally planned. Anthem University was on summer break, so there were no baseball games. High School was over, and there were no major events happening until she moved into college, and that was still two months away. Nevaeh spent most of her summer with Vinny, Rachel, Keven, and Morgan. Some days she would go for hikes with Morgan and Halo, go to the beach with Rachel, or go to the movie plex with Vinny. Nevaeh was still practicing her catching with Vinny on a daily basis too. Baseball was in her blood; she had to be the best at the sport she loved so much.

Before she knew it, she was signing up for classes online. At Anthem, students made their own schedules. Anthem counselors emailed a list of required classes, and students would sign up online. With such a high number of students, this was easier on the counselors and made perfect sense in allowing the students to make important decisions on their own. In two weeks, Nevaeh would officially be a student at Anthem University. In the meantime, Nevaeh loaded the Equinox with her belongings and moved into her dorm at Anthem. Mrs. Bennet packed some special things for Nevaeh, and Morgan and Mrs. Bennet helped Nevaeh unload the carload of her life. They soon realized that her roommate had already moved in.

"Where is she?" Morgan asked.

"Not sure, but she has a lot of stuff," Nevaeh answered.

"Yeah, she does...let's snoop around," Morgan suggested.

"NO!" Nevaeh said, "That's wrong."

Morgan looked at her. "I just want to make sure she's not some serial killer. What do you know about her?" she asked Nevaeh.

"All I know is that her name is Emma Saxxby and she's from Austin."

"Exactly," Morgan said. "She could be a serial killer."

"That's highly unlikely!" Nevaeh scowled at Morgan.

Morgan looked at her, smiled, and said, "Not if she eats cereal for breakfast."

Chapter 15

Morgan had returned home before Emma returned to the dorm. Nevaeh was told to text Morgan and tell her everything about Emma. As it turned out, Nevaeh and Emma had a lot in common. Emma was going to be playing softball in the Spring, and she heard of Nevaeh's specialized sports teens. Emma had an older brother who was also attending Anthem University. Miles Saxxby was two years older than Emma, and he had Down's Syndrome. Emma had long curly blond hair, blue eyes, plucked eyebrows, and an overall friendly face. Her brother, Miles looked just like her, but his hair was short. Emma and Nevaeh talked for hours, and Nevaeh learned how Miles loved baseball and wanted to play.

"My brother is a great guy," Emma told Nevaeh, "Just no one will give him a chance to play because of his Down's syndrome."

Nevaeh and Emma talked well into the night. Nevaeh had the goal of helping Miles join the baseball team in the back of her mind. She would make a plan when the time was right. By midnight, Morgan texted Nevaeh.

"Are you okay? You never texted me."

Nevaeh took a few minutes to answer and said, "Oh My God! You are right!"

"About what?!?" Morgan texted back.

"She's a serial killer!" Nevaeh said.

"Are you serious?" Morgan responded, worried.

"Yeah, she eats Cap'n Crunch and everything!"

Morgan never texted Nevaeh back that night.

"I guess she didn't find her own joke funny," Nevaeh thought.

The following day, Nevaeh got to meet Miles. Emma was right, and they did look similar. Miles told Nevaeh how his favorite team was The New York Yankees, and how he wanted to go to Yankee Stadium someday.

"Maybe one day, the three of us will go to a game," Emma told him. Nevaeh showed him her locket and explained how the picture inside was from Yankee Stadium.

"I also like the Texas Rangers and the New York Mets. Can we watch a Yankees game when they play them?" Miles asked.

"We can definitely look into tickets for a subway series," Emma said. Nevaeh was pleased that her roommate wasn't some slob and could relate to her. In the process of meeting Miles, Nevaeh had to explain what happened to her arm. When he blurted out that her arm was missing, Nevaeh tried to make a joke and say, "What is it?" and acted confused, but poor Miles thought she lost it and started searching for it. Emma never asked out of courtesy, but once Nevaeh was done explaining the story, they both gave her a hug and said, "I'm sorry."

The following week, the fall semester started. Nevaeh found her classes to be interesting, yet difficult. When she wasn't studying or in class, she spent a lot of time playing ball with Emma and Miles. Nevaeh would have practiced with Vinny, but he was away at college too. She was glad that she made new friends, but she couldn't wait for the holiday break so she could see Vinny, Rachel, Keven, and Morgan. She even missed Halo.

As the term continued, Halloween came and passed with candy and costumes on campus, and soon Thanksgiving arrived. Nevaeh stayed at Anthem because she had a lot of work to complete for her assignments. She missed her family and friends dearly but knew that her academics were important. Morgan's video called Nevaeh on Thanksgiving Day, and she got to see Halo, her Grandparents, and her mom, which improved her overall mood. She thought of past Thanksgiving holidays, when her dad was alive, and how much fun her family always had...and the beautiful dinners her mom cooked were better than anyone else's. She wished everyone could have a dinner like her family's. It was the best ever, and she wondered if she had made a mistake by not going home. She missed everyone terribly, and Vinny.

"It's going to be weird going Black Friday shopping without you," Morgan said.

After the video call ended, Nevaeh felt bad about not being home for the Thanksgiving feast. Later that night, Nevaeh drove to the mall to meet Morgan for the Black Friday shopping. Morgan was beyond surprised to see her older sister, and both girls spent the rest of the morning laughing and shopping. Once Nevaeh returned to the university, she barely had time to blink. The end of the semester and final exams were upon her. As always, Nevaeh completed her exams with flying colors and finally headed home for the Christmas holiday break.

When Nevaeh arrived home, she was pleased to find her grandparents were staying with them for the Christmas weekend. She had only seen her grandparents on the video call, so she embraced all the hugs and kisses. As the family tradition called for, the days leading to Christmas were spent baking cookies, and decorating the tree. When Christmas morning came, Morgan woke Nevaeh early, and the gift exchange started in earnest. Later in the evening of Christmas, Nevaeh exchanged gifts with Rachel, Keven, and Vinny. It felt great to be home, but Nevaeh knew that she would soon have to return to Anthem University. She knew that she would once again miss her friends and family, but she also knew that she was continuously getting closer to baseball season.

Chapter 16

Upon Nevaeh's return to Anthem University, she was pleased to find Emma and Miles in her dorm room.

"I'm glad you're both here!" Nevaeh told them enthusiastically. "I brought you both Christmas gifts and I have homemade cookies."

Nevaeh placed her bags on her bed and started to dig for the gifts. While she was looking for her gifts, Emma placed a wrapped gift on Nevaeh's bed, and Miles ate some of the cookies.

"We got you a gift, too," Emma said.

"These are really good cookies," Miles told her.

Nevaeh handed Emma and Miles their gifts and opened her own. Nevaeh gave Emma a pair of batting gloves for the upcoming softball season and gave Miles a New York Yankees T-shirt that has "Saxxby" on the back. Emma thanked Nevaeh for her gift, and Miles was so happy, he gave Nevaeh a hug and refused to let go.

"Nevaeh can't open her gift if you won't let her go," Emma told Miles. Miles eventually let go, and Nevaeh opened her gift. Inside the box was a picture of the three of them in a frame that Miles and Emma made.

"It was Miles's idea," Emma explained to Nevaeh.

"Do you like it?" Miles asked.

"More than like," Nevaeh answered. "I love it!"

The Spring semester was starting which meant classes were resuming. The start of Spring, however, also meant the beginning of baseball. Tryouts were quickly approaching, and Nevaeh was beyond excited.

"Come with me to tryouts," Nevaeh told Miles.

"Okay!" Miles said, and he ran to grab his glove.

Nevaeh found Marcus Fjord on the diamond and explained why she brought Miles with her.

"No one has ever given him a chance because of his Down's Syndrome. We talked last year about giving everyone a fair and equal opportunity, so I brought Miles along," she told Marcus.

"The more candidates we have, the better off we will be. Plus, you're right. Everyone deserves a chance." Marcus agreed.

Anthem had not come remotely close to the playoffs since Marcus was their ace pitcher. Marcus was instructed by George Hammerhorn to make the "smart" choices and develop a championship team. George threatened Marcus with his job if he failed to grasp a national championship. Marcus was relieved to see a large number of prospects. The only challenge left was choosing a championship-caliber team. Marcus knew that Kyle

Swabell would be in the rotation, and one of the best pitchers he had, but he still needed to find players for every other position.

As the tryouts started, Nevaeh realized that her toughest competition at catcher would be a boy named Robert McGee. Robert was an overweight boy, but he was a tremendous hitter as well. Robert's size made him good at blocking balls in the dirt. Robert kept his dark hair buzzed and had dark brown eyes. Every time Nevaeh tried to talk to him, he was very rude to her. At one point, Robert told her "I don't know why you're here. I'm a better catcher, and I hit better than you. You only have one arm, and you're a girl, besides."

Nevaeh was getting used to the rude comments, so she simply said "Really? I'm a girl? I had no idea."

Miles wanted to play shortstop since he idolized Derek Jeter, but Miles couldn't field the ball that well. When Miles batted, he made contact, but the ball didn't go very far and would have most likely resulted in an out, had they been playing a game.

Once the tryouts were over, Coach Fjord informed the players that he would be sending an email to the players who made the cut. The email was going to include the starting lineup, backups, and other odds and ends.

"Please don't flood me with emails and phone calls," Coach Fjord said. "If you made the team, there will be an email. If you don't get an email, I encourage you to try again next year."

Nevaeh headed back to her dorm room feeling confident. "I really hope I make the team. I've worked so hard," she thought.

Nevaeh refused to overthink the situation. She had learned to expect the worst like her dad taught her. She had been let down so many times, and she had seen Robert play. "The only thing I have on him is speed," she thought. Nevaeh sat by her computer hoping an email would come through.

"Are you nervous?" Emma asked.

Nevaeh looked away from her computer. "Incredibly! I just hope I make the team. Robert was good, so he could start."

Emma laughed. "But Robert can't run like you. I hope you and Miles both make the team. It will break his heart if he doesn't."

"I'm sure Coach Fjord will find a place for Miles," Nevaeh told her.

BING!

"I just got an email," Nevaeh said.

Nevaeh turned back to her computer and saw an email from Coach Fjord. The subject line was titled "Congratulations." Nevaeh's heart was pounding out of her chest! She clicked on and read the email.

"Congratulations! You have been selected to play on this year's baseball team at Anthem University. Below, I have included the starting lineup, pitching rotation, bullpen list, and backup players. Our first practice will be next Friday at 4 pm. Please arrive promptly. If you have any questions, please feel free to ask me. Coach Fjord"

The starting lineup, pitching rotation, bullpen, and backup were placed in the email as an attachment.

"I'm nervous to open the attachment," Nevaeh told Emma.

"Just open it!!" Emma squealed.

Nevaeh had butterflies in her stomach and couldn't believe she made the team. "Hopefully I'm starting," she told Emma. "I'm just glad someone is giving me a chance." Nevaeh clicked the link:

Starting Lineup
Pitching Rotation

1) Nevaeh Bennet (C)
   1) Kyle Swabell

2) Christopher Martin (RF)
   2) Phillip VanSnow

3) Brett Swann (CF)
   3) Howard Coff

4) Chadwick Zomali (1B)
   4) Garth Silinski

5) Allen Redwood (2B)

6) Alexander Pizeza (LF)

Bullpen

7) Mark Zeti (3B)

    Carlos Rivera-Son

8) Jose Rodriquez (SS)

    James Stevens

9) Pitcher

    D.J. King

Jackson Uttain

    Keith Elia

Stevie Watson

Backup players:

Robert McGee (C)	Xander McNeil (OF)	Miles Saxxby
(IF)	Scott Rasp (OF)	Reggie Botary
(IF)	Isaiah Cane (OF)	Jacoby Tarly (IF)

"OH MY GOD!" Nevaeh yelled! "I'm starting catcher! And look! Your brother made the team!" She told Emma.

Before Emma could look, Miles came bursting through the door. He had the email pulled up on his phone and the biggest smile Emma had ever seen!

"This calls for a special occasion celebration!" Emma said. "I'm ordering pizza and wings."

While Emma ordered, Miles called his mom, and Nevaeh called Rachel, Vinny, and Morgan to share the exciting news. Nevaeh worked around everyone's schedule and planned a time to meet Vinny, Rachel, Keven, and Morgan at the Moonlit Rose for a celebration dinner and milkshake. It was decided that they would all meet the following day. When the pizza and wings arrived, Nevaeh, Emma, and Miles celebrated well into the night. This was a day Nevaeh had dreamed about her entire life, and it was finally here!

Chapter 17

Part of Marcus's job as head baseball coach would be to participate in interviews with reporters. Marcus sent the team list to Marion, and the university directors as well as the team. George Hammerhorn sent the list to the local media outlets, as well as the National Sports Networks. George also took it upon himself to schedule the interview for Marcus and scheduled a separate meeting with Marcus that would take place prior to the interviews with the reporters.

Marcus arrived at George's office early and was asked to have a seat by George's secretary.

"Mr. Fjord" a sharp shrill voice called. "Come into my office, now!"

Marcus rose, gathered his belongings, and walked into George's office.

"Have you lost your mind?!" George yelled directly at Marcus.

"I am in perfect control of my senses," Marcus replied.

"It seems to me that an ape would make better choices as our baseball Coach." Hammerhorn slammed on his desk.

"And it seems to me that a chinchilla would make a better director of this University. Let's skip the jibes, and talk. Why have I been summoned?" Marcus asked.

"You know quite well why you're here. I made it perfectly clear that I did not want a cripple on our baseball team, and not only have you put a retard on our team as well. You have directly disobeyed me, and I demand an explanation!" Hammerhorn shouted.

"An explanation of my actions would be considered a courtesy, and after your use of that deplorable term, I don't believe you deserve one." Marcus shot back at Hammerhorn.

"I am a man with a First Amendment right and will speak as I please," George yelled. "Need I remind you that I am one of your supervisors? Now, again, I demand an explanation."

Marcus sighed. "An explanation is more than you deserve, but an explanation you'll get. Nevaeh Bennet doesn't hit for power, but she makes contact and is an excellent bunter. She's fast, and she is quick to recover the ball. She's a tremendous blocker, and she's mastered the art of throwing runners out at second! Considering she can do this with one arm is outstanding, and there is no reason she shouldn't be on the team."

"And what of Robert McGee!" George Hammerhorn snapped.

"Robert is talented indeed, but the facts remain that Nevaeh Bennet is an overall better player. Robert made the team; he should be grateful for that. His attitude towards Miss Bennet at tryouts would have been reason alone to cut him."

"Were you aware that Robert was offered a full scholarship to attend Paramount University and play as their starting catcher?" George asked.

"I was. I am also aware that Robert's father is Paramount's athletic director," Marcus replied.

"Well, are you aware that Robert turned down Paramount's offer because he wanted to bring Anthem their first National championship?" George asked.

"Then he should be even more grateful that I put him on the team," Marcus replied.

"Oh, that's where you are mistaken," George said. "Robert came to me and asked for approval to transfer to Paramount. I granted that request this morning. Would it be that I could transfer myself to Paramount, I would quickly be following the boy."

"Well, sir, I have to say I'm shocked!" Marcus said.

"And why are you shocked? You didn't see a player of Robert's caliber asking for a transfer to a championship-quality team? Pray, tell?"

"No, I'm shocked by the fact that for once in your career at Anthem, you've done something to improve the university. It truly is a shame that you can't follow the spoiled brat to Paramount. Are we done here?" Marcus quizzed.

George turned red with frustration. "We are NOT! You have explained your inexcusable actions with the cripple, but what of the retard?"

"I would thank you not to use that derogatory term in my presence," Marcus demanded.

"I will speak how I please, now tell me of the boy," George demanded.

"Everyone deserves a chance," Marcus said. "It is highly unlikely he will play. He is just happy to be a part of the team."

"He shouldn't be on the team at all," George roared. "I want him off the team immediately!"

"NO!" Marcus roared back.

George was as red as a firetruck. "Excuse me?" he demanded.

"I said NO. I'm the coach of this team, and Saxxby stays!" Marcus explained.

"GET OUT!" George yelled. "You have an interview to conduct."

Marcus stood and turned for the door. When he reached the door, he heard "Mr. Fjord, mark my words. At the end of the year, I will have my way. Once you fail to win a championship, we will terminate you, and I will personally remove the cripple and the retard. Now get out of my sight!"

Marcus never said another word. He simply turned, walked out the door, and closed it behind him.

"I heard some of your argument," the secretary told Marcus. "If it means anything to you, I think you did the right thing." Marcus replied with a heartfelt "Thank you!"

The secretary's comments improved Marcus's mood, and just in time. Marcus had to answer questions from reporters in less than five minutes. As Marcus approached the conference room, he could hear the chatter of all the reporters. When Marcus reached the podium, questions started flying from all directions.

"Please, one at a time," Marcus said.

The first question was, "Is it true that you have elected to start a crippled girl as catcher?"

Marcus sighed. "It is true that I have selected a very talented athlete to start as our catcher. To refer to this individual as anything other than talented is deplorable, and I will field no more questions on that matter."

"What about the Downs Syndrome boy?" Another reporter called out.

"Everyone deserves an opportunity to play. If simply-minded people can be offered a chance to be a reporter, why can't a boy be offered a chance to play ball?"

"Some say that you don't care about a championship, is that true?" another reporter asked.

"Of course, I would love to lead our team to our first National Championship, but winning isn't everything," Marcus replied.

Marcus spent an hour answering questions related to the previous three. The last question of the night was Marcus's favorite, however.

"It has been reported that one of the directors is displeased with your decision-making. What is your take on this?"

Marcus laughed. "Let him be disappointed. I'm doing my job to the best of my ability while trying to make Anthem University a better place. If those actions displease him, then maybe he shouldn't be one of our directors. What he fails to remember is that it is not the number of championships we have that defines us. How we conduct ourselves with victory or failure is what defines who we are."

With that, Marcus turned and walked away from the podium. As Marcus left the building and walked towards the parking lot, he encountered the reporters once more. "We are not done asking you questions," one of the reporters yelled. "Well, I'm done answering them," Marcus thought as he continued to walk toward his car in silence. When Marcus got to his vehicle, he reached into his pocket, grabbed his keys, and unlocked the car door.

As Marcus opened the door, he heard a question that made him freeze. Marcus knew that voice all too well. He turned and saw George standing with the reporters.

"You said that you would field no more questions on the catcher, but I implore you to justify benching one of the nation's top prospects at catching, and then allowing that same prospect to transfer to our competing university," George Hammerhorn said.

Marcus felt his cheeks flush and could feel his frustrations rising.

"You know damn good and well that I knew nothing of Robert's transfer until an hour ago. His transfer to Paramount was your doing, so do me a kindness and look for a scapegoat elsewhere. As I have already told you, and I will be more than happy to announce in front of these reporters; Nevaeh Bennet has more heart than any other player who steps foot on the diamond. Not only does she show superb dedication to the sport, but she also has more talent than most of the players on the field." Marcus stated.

"And what will you be saying when we fail to win a national title yet again?" George protested.

"Again, you have already decided the outcome of a championship that has yet to be played simply because you do not like the players I have chosen. Anyone who feels that I have selected a failing team, by all means, has the right to stay home and cheer for another team. In all honesty, if you feel my efforts have been for naught, then I implore you to look elsewhere for a team to cheer. Any negativity and jibes towards my team of players are unwanted and unnecessary. Those who are true Anthem supporters are encouraged to attend our games and cheer on all of our players. With all that being said, I encourage all of you to allow the players and the scoreboard to do the talking from this point on."

Marcus ended the impromptu interview session on that note. He sat in his vehicle, started the engine, and drove to the Moonlit Rose. All those questions made him hungry.

Chapter 18

On Saturday, Nevaeh picked Morgan up around four, and they headed to The Moonlit Rose for a celebration. Vinny, Rachel, and Keven were already there and were seated in Nevaeh's favorite booth by the jukebox. Vinny saw Nevaeh pull into the parking lot through the window and put a quarter into the jukebox. On their first date, Nevaeh told Vinny that her favorite music genre was country and that her favorite artist was Tim McGraw. When Nevaeh entered The Moonlit Rose, the song "Just To See You Smile" was playing. Once Nevaeh heard it, she instantly smiled.

"It worked!" Vinny told her as she sat down.

"What worked?" Nevaeh asked.

"The song. It made you smile," Vinny said smirking. "I'd do anything to see you smile."

"You're so corny," Nevaeh said.

As the five of them sat around and shared stories, Nevaeh looked up from her menu and noticed Coach Fjord entering the diner.

"That's my coach," Nevaeh told her friends.

If Coach Fjord noticed Nevaeh in the corner, he showed no indication. He sat in a booth at the opposite end of the diner and read over the menu. Other than noticing him walk in, Nevaeh paid him no attention. The five friends ordered their food and continued to share stories. Morgan couldn't join the college stories, but she shared stories about Halo and her sophomore year of high school.

Just as Nevaeh and her friends were finishing their meals, a loud group of friends entered the diner.

"You have to be kidding me," Nevaeh said.

"What is it?" Rachel asked.

That's Robert McGee and his friends." Nevaeh told them. "He's the one I beat for starting catcher and treated me like crap at tryouts."

"Do you want me to say something to him?" Vinny asked.

"No, leave him be," Nevaeh said.

Nevaeh tried her hardest to ignore Robert and pretend that she never noticed him, but that was quickly proving to be impossible. Robert noticed her at once and began making comments. His friends joined in, and soon the entire diner could hear them making fun of her.

"She only has one arm; how can she be a starting catcher?" she heard one of them say.

"She's really ugly," another one said.

The insults kept coming, and Vinny was starting to lose his patience.

"Just let it go," Nevaeh kept telling Vinny.

Nevaeh kept looking at Coach Fjord, but if he was listening, he showed no sign of acknowledgment. Finally, Morgan snapped.

"Shut up you fat pig!" Morgan yelled at Robert. "You're just jealous that my sister is better than you!"

Robert didn't say a word back. He just turned red. Nevaeh said that she'd had enough and told her friends it was time to leave.

"We can go back to my house," Morgan said.

They all agreed, and Rachel, Nevaeh, and Morgan went outside of the diner while Vinny and Keven went to the counter to pay.

As Nevaeh was walking towards her Equinox, she quickly learned that Robert and his friends followed.

"Hey, Freak!" Robert said as he grabbed her wrist and turned her around.

Nevaeh wrenched free from Robert's grasp and said, "I would thank you not to touch me, or speak to me!"

"I will speak to the sideshow freak if I please," Robert told her. "How about giving me a kiss to apologize for stealing my position?"

"Eww!" Morgan interjected.

"I'm not kissing you," Nevaeh told him. "Now go away and leave us alone!"

"I'm getting that kiss," Robert insisted.

Robert proceeded to grab Nevaeh's wrist again. As soon as his finger made contact, Nevaeh heard a loud SMACK and looked up. Morgan had slapped Robert so hard that there was an imprint of her hand on his left cheek.

"Keep your hands off of my sister!" Morgan yelled.

Robert looked at Morgan. He was furious! "You little bitch!" he yelled as he shoved Morgan to the ground. Robert stepped over Morgan and looked as if he was going to hit her, but Nevaeh stepped in between them.

"Move!!" Robert demanded.

When Nevaeh refused to move, Robert raised his fist. Nevaeh closed her eyes and waited for the impact. The punch never came. When Nevaeh opened her eyes, she saw that Vinny had left the diner, and grabbed Robert's fist before he could swing. Robert turned and stood nose-to-nose with Vinny. Keven put his arms around Rachel.

"You have some nerve," Robert told Vinny.

"I suggest you get out of here if you know what's good for you," Vinny said.

Robert laughed. "Good for me? Look around, there's four of us and one of you." His friends started to laugh as well.

Vinny was unmoved. "Last chance," he said. "Leave or..."

Before Vinny could finish his sentence, Robert punched him in the jaw. Vinny barely moved, and quick as lightning, Vinny landed a punch to Robert's temple with his right hand. Vinny hit Robert so hard that Robert staggered and fell to the ground.

"That one was for Morgan," Vinny yelled. "Want some more?"

Suddenly Vinny was fighting all four of them. Fists were flying everywhere. Nevaeh was surprised that Vinny was able to take on all four of them. Vinny was strong, but the numbers eventually took over. Vinny ended up on the ground while the four boys kicked. Morgan grabbed one of Nevaeh's bats out of the Equinox. "This should equal things out!" she said. Morgan never did get a chance to swing the bat.

"ENOUGH!" a voice shouted.

Nevaeh looked and saw Coach Fjord throwing the four boys off Vinny.

"Come to protect your cripple?" Robert asked.

"Seems like your old coach wants a whoopin' too!" one of the boys said.

Vinny had managed to do a number on the four boys. They all had split lips, and Robert was starting to bruise around his eyes.

"If I were you, I'd get out of here before the police show up," Marcus told the boys.

"Might be we kick your ass first!" Robert bellowed.

"I invite you to try," Marcus replied with a smirk.

Robert took a step forward, but Vinny had returned to his feet, and Morgan stood behind them with a baseball bat in hand. Robert thought better of the situation and left with his friends.

"Are you alright?" Marcus asked Vinny. "That was a noble thing you did protecting the girls and all."

"Thank you," Vinny replied. "Just a few scrapes," he laughed.

Marcus turned towards Nevaeh and asked for a minute of her time.

"You've got yourself a fierce little sister," he laughed, "and a good boyfriend."

"Thank you!" Nevaeh replied.

I just want you to know that you're probably going to hear a lot of crap from spectators, and other teams. Are you prepared for that?" Marcus asked.

"I've been waiting my entire life for this opportunity," Nevaeh said. "I always knew I could face criticism because I am a girl. When I lost my arm, I knew then too. It will only make me stronger. Trust me, Coach, I'm ready."

"Okay, Good!" Marcus said. "Make sure you tell me if Robert contacts you again."

"I will," Nevaeh said.

Chapter 19

The next time Nevaeh saw her coach was the following weekend at the team's first practice. Coach Fjord had found a boy named Anthony Westers to replace Robert McGee as the backup catcher. He wasn't as good as Robert, but he was a lot nicer. Coach Fjord took all the players and simulated gameplay as practice. Nevaeh got to catch for every pitcher on the team. Coach Fjord told her it would be important to know each pitcher, especially the starters. Coach Fjord had previously been a starting pitcher for Anthem, and he was teaching all the pitchers how to throw as curveball as he could. Kyle Swabell was the best at the curve, and his fastball was incredibly fast. Out of all the pitchers on the team, Nevaeh struggled to catch his the most. Especially the curveball. Although Nevaeh caught all the pitches, she spent most of her time with Kyle.

"I want you and Kyle to become accustomed to each other. Your chemistry together will determine the outcome of our games. When we need a win, he'll be your starting catcher," Coach Fjord told her.

Nevaeh also worked with all the pitchers and Coach Fjord to develop signs. Nevaeh was short a hand, so she would pat the dirt, or move her glove left to right to signal a pitch, instead of using original signs. They developed other signs as well. They had accomplished a lot at their first practice, and Nevaeh felt comfortable with all her teammates. Everyone treated her like an equal. Nevaeh was actually relieved that Robert was no longer on the team. This was the first time in a long time that Nevaeh felt like she belonged.

Before the practice was over, Coach Fjord went over some signs and terminology.

"We're going to want to strike first. Nevaeh is our fastest runner, which is why she bats first. Contact and speed. The goal will be for Nevaeh to get on base, and Christopher who is our second-best bunter will hit second. Ideally, Nevaeh will use her speed to steal second, and I will give Christopher the sign to bunt if necessary. A successful bunt would put Nevaeh on third easily. Chadwick and Brett both hit for power, so that will increase the likelihood of a Sac Fly, or Homerun, and we should score first. Any questions?" Marcus asked. When no one raised their hands, he continued.

"Obviously, the goal is to take on early lead, and leave the rest up to our starting pitchers."

After a few more practices, Coach Fjord was able to simulate everyone's stats.

"By the look of things early on, our starting pitchers have ERA's below two, and our averages are through the roof. Along with our on-base percentages, I don't see how we wouldn't be championship caliber," Marcus told them.

The following week, the baseball season officially started. Anthem's first game was Wednesday night at their home stadium. As the rest of the team prepared for the game, Nevaeh sat in the locker room. "This is it," she thought to herself. "I've waited for this moment my entire life, and now that it's here, I'm incredibly nervous."

Kyle entered the locker room and saw Nevaeh on the bench.

"Are you ready?" he asked her.

"I'm ready," she said. "And nervous."

Kyle chuckled. "Don't be nervous. You'll do fine, I've seen you play."

"Thanks, but that doesn't make the butterflies go away," she told him.

"I don't know if it will mean anything to you, but I'm really glad that you'll be my catcher," Kyle told Nevaeh.

"Why is that?" she asked.

"This is my fourth year pitching at Anthem, and I've never thrown to a player who is as good as you are."

Nevaeh blushed. "Thank you!"

"Listen there's one more thing you should know," Kyle said.

"Okay..." Nevaeh replied hesitantly.

"You're going to hear things while you're batting. People in the crowd are going to yell things and say you don't belong. The other team is going to say the same while they bat. Just ignore them to the best of your ability, and let your talent do the talking."

Nevaeh nodded. "I know. I'm expecting that."

"Also," Kyle added, "I've seen these enough times, but be careful at the plate. The other team's pitchers will throw to hit you for no reason other than you are a girl."

"Really?" Nevaeh asked. "I can handle a hit," she said as she shrugged.

"Well, if they hit you on purpose, just know that I've got your back and I'll hit their next batter in return," Kyle told her.

"If they hit me on purpose, I'm going to make them regret it when I steal and score," Nevaeh said laughing.

Kyle laughed and said, "That's a good attitude to have! Let's warm up."

Nevaeh was surprised with the standing ovation she received as she squatted behind the plate. The home side bleachers were filled with Anthem students holding signs that read

Some signs even read that she was making history. Although there was applause and support from the home side, she could hear snickering from the away bleachers and the other team. Most of what she could hear was "How is she supposed to catch with one arm?" or "What was Fjord thinking to allow a girl a starting position, let alone a handicap?" Nevaeh ignored the jests and thought "I'll show them."

Before the game started, Nevaeh kept looking at the signs that read "Nevaeh Bennet #4." She wondered why Coach Fjord gave her number four. He allowed everyone else to pick their numbers, and he wore number twenty-six, but why didn't she have a choice? When she asked Coach Fjord why he assigned her number four, all he told her was that it was a significant number…but why?

Suddenly, the umpire yelled "Play Ball!" and everyone took their positions on the diamond. The first batter that approached the plate did exactly what Kyle said they would. "Try not to drop the ball," he told Nevaeh. Nevaeh just ignored him. Kyle threw the first pitch, swing, and miss.

"Strike one!" The umpire yelled.

The next pitch delivered the same outcome.

"Strike two!"

Nevaeh heard the batter grunt and said, "Maybe you should be a little less concerned about my catching skills and focus more on hitting the ball."

The batter turned, gave her a nasty look, and proceeded to strike out. The next batter swung on the first pitch and popped the ball straight up into the air. Nevaeh caught it easily for our number two. The third batter had more patience than the previous two and took the first two pitches for ball one, and ball two. He swung on pitch three and hit it directly into Jose's glove at shortstop. With that, the teams switched sides, and it was Nevaeh's turn to bat.

As Nevaeh walked toward the plate, she realized that the pitcher was the boy who told her not to drop the ball. "If Kyle's right, he might try to hit me," she thought. Nevaeh didn't know his name, but the back of his Jersey said "Game." "That must be his last name," she thought.

The first pitch was a fastball. Nevaeh could hear it cutting through the air, but she also noticed it was coming directly towards her face. She ducked, and she heard it hit the net behind them.

"Ball!" the umpire yelled.

"Note to self, remember to ask about this "Game" fellow when I get back to the dugout," Nevaeh said to herself.

Game threw the next pitch and again Nevaeh moved out of the way.

"Ball two!"

"Come on up! Do your job!" she heard Kyle yell.

"He's clearly trying to hit her!" another teammate yelled.

Nevaeh even heard a fan in the home section yelling to take him out of the game.

As the next pitch came, Nevaeh once again tried to move out of the way, but there was nowhere to go. Nevaeh turned and felt the smack in the center of her back. As the sound echoed through the stadium, the home section began to "boo" the pitcher.

Nevaeh made her way to first base, and Coach Fjord came out of the dugout in a frenzy of frustration. When Nevaeh looked back from first base, she saw her coach in a heated discussion with the home plate umpire, and the other team's coach.

Nevaeh couldn't tell what Coach Fjord was saying, but she could tell by his hand gestures that he was not very happy. Coach Fjord eventually went back into the dugout and play resumed.

"If they hit me on purpose, I'm going to make them regret it," Nevaeh thought, remembering her conversation with Kyle. She studied Game as he pitched to Christopher. The first pitch to Christopher was a ball, and all Nevaeh needed to see. "You're the fastest player on the team," Coach Fjord told her of their practices.

137

"If you think you can steal, do it," she remembered him saying. As Game prepared for his next pitch, he glanced over at Nevaeh.

"I'm going to make him regret it," she thought.

Game found his footing, wound up, and released the pitch. Before the pitch could even leave his fingers, Nevaeh was off and running. Christopher saw that Nevaeh was stealing and took the pitch for a strike. The catcher caught the ball, and quickly threw to second. Nevaeh slid headfirst into second. As a dust cloud rose, the umpire yelled "SAFE!"

Nevaeh stood at second base as the home section of the bleachers went nuts. After the successful steal, Coach Fjord gave the signal for Christopher to bunt, and allow Nevaeh to advance to third base. The very next pitch, Christopher saw was a fastball down the center of the plate. Christopher squared his bat and dropped a successful bunt towards the third bast, which allowed Nevaeh to advance. The third baseman was pulled off the base to handle the bunt and threw Christopher out at first with ease. The team and home crowd applauded Christopher on his successful sacrifice bunt as he returned to the dugout.

Next to bat for Anthem was Brett Swann. Brett was very eager to earn his first RBI of the season and swing at the first pitch. Unfortunately, Brett hit a line drive right back at Game, and Game caught it for the second out. Chadwick was batting next for Anthem. Nevaeh knew that Chadwick was the best hitter on their team, so she felt confident that he would get an RBI. She lost that confidence as he swung and missed the next two pitches. The next pitch Game threw was an inside slider that Chadwick took for a ball. Nevaeh looked at Game as he wiped the sweat off his brow. "He's nervous," she thought. "That means he'll be desperate." Nevaeh knew that Game would most likely throw a breaking pitch in an attempt to get Chadwick to swing out of the Zone and strike out.

"If you think you can steal, do it," she thought.

Again, Nevaeh watched as Game found his footing, wound up, and released the pitch. Nevaeh took off running and heard the announcer say, "In an unprecedented move, Nevaeh Bennet is attempting to steal home." The crowd was hushed as Nevaeh ran. Everything seemed to be moving in slow motion. The game had thrown a curveball that went to the dirt. The break in speed allowed Nevaeh an opportunity, and the ball in the dirt only increased her odds of success. Chadwick moved back as Nevaeh slid home. The catcher gathered the ball and applied a tag to Nevaeh's side. As the dust settled, the stadium was silent.

"SAFE!" the umpire bellowed.

The crowd was electrified, and chants of "Nevaeh! Nevaeh!" were rising from the home section. Nevaeh stood with a smile on her face, looked at Game, and thought "I'll make them regret it." As Nevaeh walked back to the dugout, she received a standing ovation from the crowd. When she sat on the bench, Miles ran up to her and said, "That was amazing!"

Suddenly, Nevaeh heard a loud "CRACK". She looked up to see that Chadwick had just drilled a home run over the centerfield fence. Anthem was winning, 2 – 0.

While Nevaeh put her gear on and sat in the dugout, coach Fjord told her who Theodore Game was. Theodore was a sophomore at East View University and had everything handed to him.

"Personally, I don't think he's that good," Coach Fjord told her. "His father probably paid for his position."

Coach Fjord and Kyle also informed Nevaeh that Theodore disagreed with the team allowing her to play. Kyle had shown her a social media post where Game said, "I'm glad my school doesn't let some stupid girl play baseball." Coach Fjord told Nevaeh that she handled herself well. "Just let your talent speak for you," he told her. Once Coach Fjord walked away, Kyle told her not to worry. "I'll get some revenge for you."

The next two innings went perfectly for Anthem. East View failed to obtain one hit and went down in order every time. In between Nevaeh had another at-bat where she successfully dodged two pitches and hit a single into right field. Anthem had more hits, but they were unable to score. When the top of the fourth inning arrived, Kyle faced Game at the plate. Nevaeh made the sign to start with a curve ball, but Kyle shook his head in disagreement. When she gave the sign for a fastball, he agreed. I'll get revenge for you" she remembered him saying. Kyle found his footing, would up, and released. The pitch that Kyle threw came so fast that if you blinked, you would have missed it. Nevaeh never even got the chance to catch it. The ball hit Game in the elbow, and Game let out an agonizing cry of pain.

"You did that on purpose!" Game yelled at Kyle.

"And you hit my catcher!" Kyle yelled back.

Before an altercation could happen, the home plate umpire stepped in between them and removed them both from the game. Both coaches flew out of their respective dugouts to complain and argue, but the umpire gave them both a warning and said they would be removed from the game as well. Both coaches tucked their tails between their legs and returned to their dugouts. Coach Fjord sent D.J. King to the mound for the rest of the game, and Anthem took their first victory with a score of $2 - 1$.

Later that night, Coach Fjord got an email from George Hammerhorn that read,

"Marcus,

Kyle Swabell's actions at tonight's game were absolutely uncalled for. I have already received several phone calls from Theodore Game's father demanding that we pay the medical bill. It seems that the poor lad has suffered a fractured elbow from Anthem's resident monster. As a result, I have reassured Mr. Game that full compensation for poor Theodore's elbow will be paid directly from your salary. Furthermore, I am suspending Kyle from his next two starts. You and Kyle should be thankful that I am a kind and reasonable man. Lastly, to ensure that you obtain a better grasp on this team, I have decided to join you in the dugout henceforth. s/G. Hammerhorn"

Marcus shared that email with the team and let them know that Mr. Hammerhorn would be looking for all faults. Marcus knew why Kyle had thrown a pitch at Theodore Game and didn't blame him. Yet he could not condone the behavior and had no grounds to argue the suspension.

Anthem proceeded to lose their next six games. George had been of no assistance in the dugout and brought the team's morale to an all-time low. George was also fond of blaming Nevaeh for the losses, even though they were not her fault. The sixth game they lost was because of a catching error that Nevaeh made at home plate, however. The way George screamed and yelled at her; one would think the world was ending. Marcus could see that Nevaeh was on the verge of tears, but she never cried.

Vinny, Rachel, Keven, and Morgan attended every game and sat above the dugout.

"What was all that screaming about?" Morgan asked.

"Mr. Hammerhorn blamed me as usual for the loss," Nevaeh sighed. "And he's bound and determined to prove Coach Fjord to be a failure."

"That dude has some kind of problem," Vinny said. "He's always yelling about one thing or the other."

Nevaeh was loading her equipment into the back of her Equinox when she heard footsteps quickly approaching.

"Nevaeh!" Coach Fjord yelled as he was running towards her. Nevaeh looked at her coach and thought George had sent him to kick her off the team. She was incredibly relieved by what he said.

"Mr. Hammerhorn was out of line," Marcus said huffing from running. "I just sent an email to Mrs. Fragnoli and wanted to catch you before you left." He sighed, "Are you okay?"

Nevaeh took a deep breath. "Yeah, it just gets tiring being harped on all the time."

"I know, it's frustrating," Marcus agreed. "But you have handled yourself with dignity while he has made a fool of himself."

"He may not be so foolish," Nevaeh said.

"What do you mean by that?" Marcus asked.

"Well, I am the reason we lost our last game. I made an error when it counted most. Not to mention that Kyle was suspended because of me. Sometimes I just feel like I don't belong here. I worked so hard to get here, but I'm a girl. Maybe I just don't belong."

"Don't ever be hard on yourself" Marcus said. "You belong exactly where you are. Even the greats made errors. Do you think Yogi Berra went through his entire career without an error? He's still a Hall of Famer. You're the best catcher I've seen in a long time, and I used to pitch. As far as Kyle's suspension, he knew the risks when he threw that pitch. He protected his teammate, which means he protected his family. Other pitchers won't be as eager to throw at you knowing the team might retaliate."

During their discussion, they moved around the Equinox, and Nevaeh stood with the driver's side door open.

"May I ask what that is hanging from your rearview mirror?" Marcus asked Nevaeh.

"It's a locket my boyfriend gave me," Nevaeh said as she handed it to her coach. "There's a picture of my father and myself inside."

Marcus took the locket and opened it to look at the picture inside. "I think the right moment has arrived," he told Nevaeh as he handed the locket back.

"What moment?" Nevaeh asked, confused.

Marcus sighed. "Your father was my best friend in college. When you were little, your father and I would tell you stories of our days in baseball. He was my catcher when we made it to the National Championship Playoffs. As you grew older, you forgot the stories we shared with you, and you were developing a love for baseball. Your father decided to keep his legacy from you at that point so that you could build your own."

"But my father didn't attend college," Nevaeh said.

"That's what he wanted you to believe. He never needed his degree to be the Foreman at "Lucky Lumbers." Everything happened by chance. You're attending the same college as your father, and you're playing his position. You're even..."

..." Wearing his number," Nevaeh interrupted.

Marcus smiled. "Exactly. Everything has fallen into place the way that God intended. It's a miracle that four years ago

I wrote that I expected to see you on the diamond, and four years later here we are, and I am your coach!"

"Four years ago?" Nevaeh thought. "You're the one who sent me that anonymous get-well card," she said.

"I am" Marcus agreed.

"And you were at my dad's funeral! That's why I thought you looked familiar."

Marcus smiled. "I wondered if you would make that connection. Anyway, Mr. Hammerhorn is foolish, and the team would suffer greatly if you left. Your father kept secrets so that you could build your own legacy. You have more heart than any other player on the team, and I know your father would be proud of you."

Nevaeh smiled, with tears in her eyes, "Thank you, Coach!"

"So, I can expect to see you at tomorrow's practice? You're not going to leave the team?" Coach Fjord asked.

"I'll be there," Nevaeh said proudly.

"Good!" Coach Fjord said. "Also, since it's my job to advise you when I played, I used to wear a cross necklace as my lucky charm. It might do you good to wear the locket and have your father close at heart during the games. You're already a better catcher than he was, but who knows, he might just give you strength when you feel weak."

Nevaeh took Coach Fjord's suggestion and immediately placed the locket around her neck. Nevaeh thanked her Coach for the advice, parted ways, and drove home.

Chapter 20

Marcus did not look forward to another interview session, especially when his team's record was one and six. George Hammerhorn, however, was quite fond of watching Marcus struggle through interviews, and scheduled one, nonetheless. On the day of the interviews, Marcus found his best suit and tie and headed toward the conference room. Marcus wore a white dress shirt, black dress pants and shoes, and a navy blue blazer. He wore a black tie with a golden A in the center for Anthem University and silver cuff links that were in the shape of baseballs. As Marcus approached the conference room, he could hear the chatter of the many reporters on the other side of the double oak doors. Marcus paused outside of the doors to listen. He had hopes of hearing some questions and preparing answers.

As Marcus put his ear to one of the oak doors, George came bursting through the other.

"There you are!" George bellowed. "Get in there and stop making these wonderful people wait!"

Marcus had very little, to no time at all to respond. George was ushering him through the door, and then questions started. There were so many questions coming at once that Marcus could only hear a cluster of chatter, and the shutters of cameras.

"Please!" Marcus yelled as he reached the podium. "Please! One question at a time!"

Very slowly the chatter began to quiet down and then the first question came.

"Mr. Fjord, what can you tell us about your team's record?"

Marcus sighed. "Currently, we are not playing as well as we can. We have experienced some setbacks, and we are working on improving. We may currently be last in the Division, but several championship teams started with a losing record."

"So, you still believe that you have a championship-caliber team?" one reporter asked.

"I strongly believe we are a championship-caliber team; we just need to smooth out a few wrinkles," Marcus answered.

"What do you make of your catcher erroring and costing the last game?" was the next question.

"As I told our catcher, even Yogi Berra made errors throughout his career, and he not only had a legendary career, but was honored in Cooperstown, New York, and inducted into the Hall of Fame. Every player has made or will make errors. It's part of the game."

The next report asked, "Do you plan on keeping Nevaeh Bennet as your starting catcher after that blunder."

"That question not only is repetitive, but ridiculous. Of course, I will be keeping Miss Bennet as our starting catcher. Again, even the best has made errors."

"What do you make of Kyle Swabell and his suspension? Do you think regaining your ace will improve your record?" The next reporter asked.

"I think Kyle's return will definitely boost the team's morale. As to his suspension, I had no reason to argue. I understood Mr. Swabell's actions, but could not, and would not warrant them."

Marcus glanced at his watch and told the reporters that he had enough time to answer one more question.

"There is a rumor going around that your current catcher is the daughter of your former catcher and best friend. Some say that she made the team out of bias. If this rumor is true, why keep such information a secret?"

Marcus felt shocked. "How do you know about that?" he thought. He instantly regretted allowing one more question, but he answered anyway.

"It is true that Jason Bennet was my former catcher and best friend. It is also true that Nevaeh Bennet is Jason's daughter. However, as many of you witnessed in our first game, Nevaeh was chosen based on her talent, not because of my friendship with her deceased father. In fact, until the other night, Nevaeh had no idea that I knew her father. We kept it a secret only from her to allow her to build her own legacy. We also felt that had Nevaeh known about my own, and her father's legacy at Anthem, she would have felt obligated to play. Jason wanted her to not only build her own legacy but make her own decisions. So, to answer your question, there was absolutely no bias in selecting Nevaeh as our starting catcher. Thank you."

Marcus started to walk away from the podium, and more questions about Nevaeh and her father kept coming.

"I said no more questions," Marcus repeated as he left the conference room. Marcus remembered the ambush in the parking lot the first time he had an interview, so he waited in his office and reviewed some plays for the team to improve on. Marcus ended up spending four hours in his office as he lost track of time. The extra time in his office allowed him to develop plans to bring to the players at practice, and as he walked to his car, all the reporters were gone.

Chapter 21

The team's next practice went incredibly well. Kyle had returned from his suspension, and the rest of the team appeared to find their confidence once more.

"I know it sounds stupid but wearing the locket and keeping the picture of my dad close to my heart makes me feel more comfortable. Thank you for the suggestion," Nevaeh told Marcus.

Marcus had gone over the faults that each player showed in the previous six games and worked individually to fix each fault. He was pleased to see the team improving and working well together. Nevaeh's appreciation also helped Marcus's mood.

"I think we will be ready for tomorrow's game," Marcus announced to the team. "Everyone has improved, and I'm confident we will get the win."

The team cheered in agreement with Marcus's announcement. As with all national college sports, travel was required. Tomorrow's away game for Anthem was in Florida. The University booked the hotel rooms, and the team loaded their equipment onto their tour bus as soon as practice ended. The ride to Florida lasted several hours, but once they arrived at their hotel, Nevaeh was relieved to find that she had her own room. Between the practice and travel, she was exhausted. Once she got to her room and lay on the bed, she quickly fell asleep.

The following morning, the team gathered for breakfast in a party room that was designated for them. There was a buffet set up with pancakes, waffles, sausage, bacon, eggs, and fruit. Pitchers of orange juice, milk, and apple juice were on all the tables. The members of the Anthem baseball team ate quickly, thanked their host, and boarded the bus. The Florida coach told Marcus that they could arrive early to warm up and practice. Marcus had every intention of taking advantage of that offer.

"It looks like it's going to rain," Nevaeh told her coach.

"That's just Florida weather," Marcus responded. "Some people have reported downpours in the front yard, while their back yard remained sunny and dry."

Nevaeh laughed and boarded the bus. As they drove to the field, Nevaeh watched the grey clouds gather and swirl outside the windows.

"I still think it's going to rain," Nevaeh told Kyle. "Those clouds look angry." Kyle laughed. "Coach said there is no chance of rain. He looked up the forecast. Plus, if it did storm, it would only last a few minutes."

They couldn't have been on the diamond for more than twenty minutes when Nevaeh felt the first raindrop hit her cheek. She looked at her coach as if to say, "I told you so," but he insisted the rain would soon cease. Within three minutes it was pouring down, and lightning cracked across the sky. All the players on the team ran to the dugouts to stay dry.

"It will pass," Coach Fjord kept on insisting. Fifteen minutes later Coach Fjord received a call letting him know that the game was delayed until tomorrow due to rain, thunder, and lightning. The team had to trudge through a field that had turned to mud in order to get back to the bus. All the while, Nevaeh looked at her coach and said, "Told you so," and trotted off to the bus.

The game was scheduled for the next day and Marcus decided to let his team rest at the hotel.

"The game has been rescheduled for noon, so rest up! We will be boarding the bus at ten thirty. I recommend eating breakfast, but that's your choice," Marcus announced.

The morning of the game, Nevaeh, Kyle, and Miles sat together as usual. Nevaeh and Kyle discussed pitches and signals, and Miles would confirm or deny their ideas. Nevaeh and Kyle felt good, including him, and he did have some good suggestions. The field crew was still working on repairing the field when they arrived. The storm had really done a number. The home plate was completely covered by water. The field crew kept adding dirt and raking. Once it was smoothed out, they would repeat the process until everything was perfect. Finally, the foul lines were painted, and the teams were permitted to warm up. The Florida Flippers, whose mascot was a shark, took the field first.

Since this was an away game, Anthem would be batting first. The umpire yelled "Play Ball!" and Nevaeh walked out of the dugout and to the plate. "His name is Ethan Fish," Nevaeh thought. "The best pitcher Florida has, and his best pitch is the fastball and slider."

Nevaeh stood in the batter's box, hoisted her bat, and waited for the first pitch. The first pitch was a fastball, and it was so fast, she never even saw it. The next pitch was also a strike, and she swung and missed at the third. Nevaeh put her head down and walked back to the dugout.

By the third inning, she didn't feel as ashamed for striking out. Anthem was hitless, and Ethan only needed to get Kyle out for a perfect three-inning. The entire game was Kyle versus Ethan so far. Both teams were hitless. Granted, it was still early in the game, but hitless, nonetheless. Kyle looked at two balls, and then a third. Coach Fjord gave the signal for the "green light," meaning Kyle was free to swing for the fences. The next pitch was a fastball that was just over the corner of the plate. Kyle swung and connected with the ball. The ball flew to the gap between the left and center fielder. The ball rolled to the wall before the centerfielder even grabbed it. By then, Kyle was rounding second and heading for third. The throw came quickly, and Kyle slid into third. "SAFE!" the ump yelled. Kyle had hit Anthems' first hit of the night, and it was a triple. Nevaeh was next, and there was a runner in scoring position.

"We can't hit for a sac fly, so do you want me to drop a bunt and run The Squeeze Play?" she asked Coach Fjord.

"Too risky. Try for a base hit," he answered.

It was already hard enough to hit a ball at the speed Ethan was throwing them, let alone with one arm. Nevaeh grabbed the locket around her neck, closed her eyes, and thought of her dad. When she opened her eyes, she grabbed her bat and walked to the plate.

The first pitch Nevaeh saw was another fastball. "STRIKE ONE!"

"Wait," Nevaeh thought. "He keeps throwing fastballs down the center of the plate." Nevaeh had just realized that Ethan thought she was an "easy out" and was only throwing fastballs.

"I'll show him," she thought. The next pitch was in the same exact spot as all the other pitches Nevaeh had seen him throw. She squared her bat and swung with her one arm. CRACK! The ball was lined to right field and landed right in front of the right fielder. As the ball passed the first baseman, he leaped trying to catch it, but it was out of reach.

"And Anthem's freshman catcher hits a single to right field and earning her first RBI of the year!" the stadium announcer reported.

Nevaeh looked at her dugout and saw everyone cheering, but nobody was as happy as Miles. "He might be more excited than me," she thought.

That was the best moment of the game. Kyle gave up four hits, but none were able to score. Anthem's bats stayed silent as Ethan upped his game, but the early rally gave Anthem the win with a score of 1 – 0.

After the game, the team boarded the bus, all loaded with their gear and suitcases, and traveled back to Anthem University. Nevaeh had been more excited than she had ever been, and the entire team knew it. Her base hit was the play that decided the game. Everyone congratulated her, and it's all they talked about for the entire trip home.

They finally arrived back at Anthem well into the night. The players grabbed their belongings and headed off to their dorms. Some had classes the following day, but they would all have practice. Coach Fjord insisted that everyone get a good night's rest. Nevaeh had other plans than resting, however.

As soon as she reached her dorm room, she woke Emma to tell her everything. Once she was done with Emma, she called Vinny and told him how she had hit the game-winning RBI, and how the locket was her good luck charm. By the time she had finished talking to Vinny, the sun was slowly peaking over the horizon and shining through her windows.

"Wow! Morning already," Nevaeh thought.

Nevaeh proceeded to prepare for the day and trotted off to her first class which was human anatomy. Nevaeh found the day's lesson, and her professor to be incredibly boring, and found herself sleeping and drooling onto her textbook. As the rest of the class was dismissed, Nevaeh was still asleep. Her professor picked up a textbook and dropped it on the desk next to Nevaeh's head. Nevaeh woke with a start and looked around.

"I'm sure that Coach Fjord will be thrilled to learn that his star catcher is sleeping during lessons," her professor said.

"I'm sorry, it's just..."

"I know what it is," her professor interrupted. "Your team arrived back to campus late last night, no fault of your own. For that, I will forgive you this once, but see to it that this sleeping mishap never occurs again during my lecture. I expect you to read pages 70 through 109 in your textbook and be caught up by our next class. You may be dismissed."

Nevaeh thanked her professor, gathered her belongings, and returned to her dorm. Nevaeh kept her schedule light and elected to take the three-hour lectures because they were only held once a week. She only had one class Monday through Friday in the morning, and one additional class in the afternoon on Wednesdays. Since Human Anatomy was held on Mondays, Nevaeh decided she would catch up on sleep until practice that evening.

Unfortunately, Nevaeh slept through her alarm and arrived at practice fifteen minutes late.

"Miss Bennet, so nice of you to join us," Coach Fjord announced as she walked onto the field. "Oversleeping I presume?"

Nevaeh's cheeks turned rose-colored. "No... I uh...had some issues with my car," she said.

Coach Fjord looked at her, then over at her Equinox, and back to her.

"If you say so, but I am no fool," he said. "You might want to go into the locker room and replace your pajama bottoms with your uniform pants."

Nevaeh blushed and looked down. "I'm such a fool," she thought.

Nevaeh headed towards the locker room but stopped to tell her coach she was sorry. "There's no point in lying," she said. "I fell asleep and overslept."

Coach Fjord merely laughed and told her it was alright, and to hurry and change. "We need a catcher for practice," he said.

"I was in such a hurry I forgot to change my clothes," she thought as she exited the locker room. "Well, that's behind me now. Baseball is the priority now." Nevaeh took her place behind the plate and the team had another successful practice.

"Remember, home game at six tomorrow night. No oversleeping!" Coach Fjord said laughing.

Chapter 22

The next night, Anthem hosted a team from Alabama. Kyle had pitched the previous game, and due to rotation rules, Phillip VanSnow was going to be the starting catcher. When Coach Fjord explained the rotation rules, he made it known that they were not real rules. Coach Fjord's Rotation Rule was simply to ensure that each pitcher got the rest they deserved. Marcus did not want any of his players to suffer through the same agony he did when he was their age. Marcus told his team he would have the pitchers pitch back-to-back games only when necessary. For this game, the only change was the pitcher; the rest of the lineup remained the same.

When the umpire yelled "PLAY BALL!" the players took their positions. Nevaeh went to home plate as usual and awaited the first batter. Nevaeh had worked with all the pitchers on the team and knew that Phillip's best pitches were a two-seam fastball and a charge-up. In the last game Phillip pitched, Nevaeh called for too many curveballs and he gave up three home runs, earning Anthem a loss. Nevaeh was determined to make better calls this time. As the first batter approached the batter's box, Nevaeh gave the signal to start with a low, inside, four-seam fastball. Phillip agreed and threw the pitch. When the ball snapped into the leather of Nevaeh's glove, she thought the pitch was slightly low. As she caught it, she gingerly raised her glove into the strike zone hoping the umpire would call a strike, rather than a ball.

"STRIKE ONE!"

On the next pitch, Nevaeh gave the sign for an elevated two-seam fastball. Phillip threw "snap".

"STRIKE TWO!"

Nevaeh wanted to help Phillip get a strike out, so she gave the signal for a change-up through the center of the plate. When Phillip agreed and threw the pitch, the batter's eyes grew to the size of eggs. He swung and missed.

"STRIKE THREE!"

The rest of the batters that Phillip faced that night met a similar fate. The change of speed proved to be Phillip's strength as he only allowed two hits during the entire game. Alabama was unable to score, so Phillip threw a complete shutout. Not only had Phillip and Nevaeh upped their game, but the bats of Anthem were on fire! Every player had at least one hit. Chadwick had hit a two-run homer in the fourth, and Allen Redwood seated Alabama's fate when he hit a grand slam in the seventh. The seventh was Anthem's best inning. Nevaeh started the inning with a single and stolen base. Christopher walked next, and Brett was hit by a pitch. Chadwick was looking for his second home run of the game but struck out swinging. Then Allen hit the grand slam and Alexander and Mark both hit back-to-back home runs.

Alabama finally got the three outs but gave up six total runs in one inning. Add in Chadwick's two-run shot and Anthem won, 8 – 0.

Vinny, Rachel, and Morgan took note that they hadn't heard any yelling from George Hammerhorn in the dugout. And of course, Keven didn't either, being deaf. George stayed quiet when the team was winning. He knew he would look like a fool if he yelled, but he also knew he looked foolish for doubting the team in the first place. As Anthem continued to play and win, George stayed in his office during games rather than wasting his time in the dugout.

"Where's Mr. Hammerhorn?" Garth Silinski asked one day. "I sent Mrs. Fragnoli an email and Mr. Hammerhorn sent me one saying the team is doing better, and that he had more important work to do in his office," Marcus replied.

"More like Mrs. Fragnoli told him to back off," Nevaeh said.

Overall, the team had never looked better. After the blowout where Anthem won 8 - 0, they proceeded to win the next sixteen games which gave Anthem an overall record of 19 – 6. With the season half completed, Anthem looked like a serious contender for the National title. Nevaeh and her pitchers not only gained trust between one another, but they had a chemistry that could not be matched. When Marcus had his half-season performance review, Marion and the directors were quite pleased, save George Hammerhorn.

"The directors and I are quite pleased with the team's performance this year," Marion Fragnoli told Marcus.

"Speak for yourself," George muttered.

Marion gave George a look and continued speaking.

"With the exception of dear George here, the rest of the directors and I have submitted an application on your behalf for the National Coach of the Year award. We included a letter explaining how you went out of your way and took large amounts of criticism to not only make Anthem an inclusive environment but to offer opportunities that others would not."

Marcus was stunned. "Thank you!" he said. "This means more than you can imagine."

"Do not start accepting something you have yet to win," George interrupted. "I would be shocked if the National Sports Council selected you as Coach of the Year. I'll have you know that I have also written a letter to the sports commissions, and I will be tickled pink when they look elsewhere for their Coach of the Year. And furthermore..."

"...oh, George, simmer down," Marion interrupted. I swear your anger and negativity grow with each meeting we have." Marion looked back at Marcus.

"Never mind Mr. Hammerhorn's negativity. You have the rest of our support, and we look forward to seeing what you and your team can accomplish with the remainder of the season. As far as your evaluation goes, you have been highly scored by all directors except one. The policy states that we are not allowed to disclose who fails an employee, but I'm sure you can imagine which one of us it was. Regardless, you have passed. The directors and I would like to thank you for your dedication to Anthem and wish you luck as we approach the end of the season."

"Thank you," Marcus replied. "It is my hope to bring Anthem a national title."

"And we are sure you and your team will do your hardest," Marion replied.

Marcus left the director's conference office and headed to the baseball stadium to greet his team. Their next home game would begin in an hour. Marcus arrived to find his team warming up, and their opponents exiting their bus. Tonight, Anthem would face their local competition Paramount University. Anthem and Paramount were close in the standings, which meant this game was important. Robert McGee immediately started trash-talking Nevaeh and the rest of the team once he got off the bus.

"Is he fatter than before?" Kyle asked Nevaeh.

"No, that's just his gear," she replied. "Although the bus did shake as he walked."

They both laughed and ignored Robert's jibes.

"If Robert does anything funny, I'll throw a pitch at him," Howard Coff told Nevaeh. "Just say the word."

"No, no," Nevaeh said. "Let's just focus on the win, we can't afford to lose you."

"Alright, but if you change your mind, let me know," Howard insisted.

Finally, Marcus had gone over signals and plays. They took their positions on the field, and the umpire yelled, "PLAY BALL!"

Like any good rivalry, cheers and boos could be heard around the arena. Howard was throwing as good as ever and sent the first three batters down on strikes. When Nevaeh came to the plate at the bottom of the first, Robert insulted her the entire time. She had two strikes, and one ball, and Robert was distracting her. Finally, she pictured his face on the ball and hit a home run right down the foul line, and just over the fence in right field. As she came around third and headed for home, Robert looked like he had seen a ghost. The look on his face amused Nevaeh, and she giggled as she walked past.

Robert had been placed in the "clean up" position and led off the top of the second. As Nevaeh called for pitches, Howard agreed. However, Nevaeh noticed something odd about Howard's cutter and called a time-out.

"Are you okay?" She asked. "Your pitches aren't hitting like usual."

"Yeah," Howard replied. "My elbow is just a little tight. No big deal."

"Okay," Nevaeh said. "We have two strikes on him, so I'm thinking throw the curve and get him out."

"Let's do it" Howard insisted.

Nevaeh went back to home plate, crouched, and gave the sign for the curveball. Howard agreed and threw the pitch. Nevaeh had anticipated the curve to land in the usual area, but she found herself moving her glove up. Robert swung. CRACK! The ball never made it into Nevaeh's glove. She stood and watched the ball sail over the center field fence.

"Darn it!" She thought. "He answered my home run with one of his own."

When she looked back at the pitcher's mound, she noticed Howard lying on the ground, holding his elbow. Coach Fjord, Kyle, and their athletic trainer Nick were standing around him. Nevaeh ran and joined them.

"It felt like something snapped when I released the pitch," Howard told them.

"The same thing happened to me," Marcus said. "Hopefully this won't be as bad as mine was. Nick, what do you think?"

Nick gingerly grabbed Howard's arm and moved it back and forth.

"It could be a ligament tear. How bad, I don't know. A doctor would need to determine that. I would definitely take him out of the game to reduce further injury," Nick suggested.

"Put me in!" Kyle insisted.

"You just pitched two days ago, and you're needed in two more. You need your rest," Coach Fjord said.

"I can handle it," Kyle said. "Trust me, coach."

"We can't risk losing another starter, I'm sorry Kyle, but no," Coach Fjord said.

"What about D.J.?" Nevaeh asked.

He's our best reliever," Kyle interjected.

"No, he's thrown a lot of innings lately. It will have to be Carlos, and we can have Keith close it out if need be."

Howard departed the game and was taken to the hospital. Coach Fjord had Carlos Rivera-Son enter the game in relief. The remainder of the game did not go well. Carlos gave up eight runs.

Anthem kept hitting and was able to score, but in the end, Anthem lost 9 – 8.

When the team went to the hospital to check in on Howard, they learned that he suffered the very same injury Coach Fjord had suffered years before. Howard had to have the same Tommy John surgery as well. Howard would be out for the rest of the season, and half of the next. When Marcus told everyone the news, he also announced that now pitching rotation would be Kyle Swabell, Phillip VanSnow, Garth Silinski, and D.J. King.

"This means we're losing our best reliever. The four starters need to work with Nevaeh, and try to pitch as many innings as possible," Coach Fjord told his team.

Meanwhile, the team's athletic trainer had to endure George Hammerhorn's wrath. George blamed Nick and said that he should have paid more attention to the players. Marcus felt bad for Nick, but he was relieved that George had placed his displeasure elsewhere. To Marcus and the director's surprise, Nick quit the next day. Not only was the team down a starting pitcher but now they were down an athletic trainer. Marion Fragnoli asked Marcus to sit in during interviews and help decide a new Athletic trainer for the team, but Marcus was hesitant that his opinion would matter. He agreed, nonetheless.

The interview process was lengthy as they had many qualified candidates. George Hammerhorn insisted that they hire a fairly young man named Cedric Praise as the new athletic trainer. Cedric was in his late twenties and had slick black hair. He had a degree in the field but lacked experience. Marcus insisted that they hire a woman named Jordan Heart. Jordan was in her forties and had previously played softball, and acted as the athletic trainer for an out-of-state college softball team. Jordan was average height, wore glasses, and had short, auburn hair.

"Jordan is our best candidate," Marcus insisted. "She has the most experience and had wonderful letters of recommendation."

"You forgot yourself," George declared. "You are not a director at this university, and you were merely invited to join us. We have already allowed one woman to botch our team, I do not intend to allow another to do the same."

Marcus ignored George and spoke to the other directors.

"It goes without saying that Anthem has come a very long way this year alone. The University has become more inclusive, and the decision to have, and allow Nevaeh to play on our team has paid off. I firmly believe that Jordan would be a huge asset to our team. Additionally, she moved to Texas from Arizona. She has heard of all our breakthroughs and decided to apply here. And rightly so. She is the best candidate, what would it say about our university to hire someone else based on her gender?"

George was the first to rebuff.

"Cedric Praise's father has been a dear friend of mine for nearly thirty years. He has also been the first to write checks and contribute generous donations to our university. It would serve as a grave insult to hire a woman for a man's sport instead of his son.
"

It was clear that the position would come down to Jordan or Cedric, but who? Marion spoke with each director privately and considered each of their reasonings. Finally, a choice had been made. Marion stood and addressed Marcus and the directors.

"After speaking with all of you, and hearing your concerns, I believe the wisest choice would be to keep our university contributors happy."

George began to smile.

"However," Marion continued. "Wise choices are not always the right choices. The right choice in this situation would be to hire the person that will help take Anthem to the next level and keep Anthem on the right path."

Marion looked at her secretary and said, "Please give Jordan Heart a call and offer her the Athletic Trainer position."

With those words, Marcus began to smile as George's smile faded.

Chapter 23

Marcus introduced Jordan to the team at their next practice. Everyone took an instant liking to her. After hearing of Howard's injury, Jordan used time at the practice to teach stretches and other exercises.

"I know some seem stupid, or dorky. But these will help prevent injuries," Jordan told them.

"Marcus took Jordan's advice and made pre-practice, and pre-game stretches mandatory. However, making them mandatory was not necessary. The team already loved Jordan and took her advice to "heart", pardon the pun.

"You did an awesome job with getting Ms. Heart hired," Nevaeh told Marcus at practice one day.

"Well, I think Coach has a crush on her," Kyle added, coyly.

Marcus gave Kyle a look as if to say, "Seriously?" but then proceeded to thank Nevaeh for the comment and walked away.

As the season continued to progress, Anthem stayed in rhythm. D.J. King was excelling as a starting pitcher and was even pitching better than Garth and Phillip. Coach Fjord was seriously considering moving D.J. into the second position on the starting rotation. Anthem continued their winning streak, but fell short every time they played Paramount, which was five more times that season, and dismally, lost all those games. At each game, Robert would gloat and prance around as if he was God's gift to baseball. Anthem's record for divisional play was extraordinary, except for when it came to games against Paramount. They were zero and six against Paramount but had no more than one loss against other division rivals.

Overall, when the regular season ended, Anthem had an overall record of 39 – 11. They were tied with the Florida Flippers and would face them in an elimination "wild card" matchup. Paramount University had an overall record of 41 – 9 and had already advanced to the semifinals for the national championship. Paramount would either be facing Anthem, or the Florida Flippers in a three-game set to determine which team would play for the national championship.

On the other divisional bracket, The New York Elementz were waiting to see if they would be facing the Ohio Otters or the New Jersey Penguins. Either way, the national championship was narrowed down to six teams.

National Championship Bracket

Southern Division	Northern Division

Anthem Wolfpack	??	**Ohio Otters**
vs	**National Champ**	vs
vs		
Florida Flippers	**Paramount Owls**	
NY Elementz	**NJ Penguins**	
(1 set)	**(Set of 3)**	**(Set of 5)**
(Set of 3)	**(Set of 1)**	

"We have done a great job thus far," Marcus announced to the team. "I have just received the official bracket for the National championship. In four days, we will face The Florida Flippers in a single-game elimination. I imagine that their ace Ethan Fish will be pitching for them. I will be putting Kyle in as our starter that day. Should we win this game, we will have two days of rest until we play our rivals, Paramount University. Kyle, I'm asking that you work with Jordan and be ready to start that series. Regardless of whether we win or lose, D.J. will start the second game, and if game three is needed, we will assess that situation once it arises."

174

"We have not been able to beat Paramount once." José asked, "What do we do about that?"

Coach Fjord smiled. "I'm glad you asked. What we do is dig down deep here." He pointed to his heart. "We have also seen their pitching, and Nevaeh knows first-hand what Robert will call pitches. Talk to her about what to expect, and we should surprise them. Likewise, they know our pitchers. I want all pitchers to work with Nevaeh, develop new signs, and new strategies."

"Sounds like a plan, Coach!" Nevaeh yelled out.

Over the next four days, Nevaeh worked with all the pitchers, but with Kyle the most. Nevaeh even had Vinny come to practices so that more pitchers could practice at once. As the elimination wild card game approached, Marcus and the rest of the team felt confident. Members of the team were able to reserve up to six seats for family and friends, and Nevaeh took advantage of the offer. She tried to get them seats by her team's dugout, but she could only get them seats behind home plate. Those seats would be reserved for the entire college world series. Family and friends maintained the same seats regardless of the stadium. It was quite a hassle, but the National Sports Administration handled those details. Coach Fjord won a coin toss, and the elimination game would be held at Anthem. Since Paramount had a better record, the first two games will be held there, and if a third game is needed, it will be held either at Anthem or in Florida, depending on which team advanced. The National Sports Administration has a specific field in South Carolina where they host all five games of The National Championship.

Nevaeh's grandparents, mother, Morgan, Vinny, and Rachel had told Nevaeh that they were leaving their schedules open for the entire world series.

"You don't even know if we will make it that far," Nevaeh said.

"Shut up!" Morgan replied...with a grin.

"You'll make it," Vinny said, pointing to her locket. "You have that."

"And heart, your whole team has heart!" Rachel interjected.

Nevaeh knew there was no point in arguing, so she gave everyone a hug and said, "Thank you!"

Emma had similar reactions and found out that her family would be seated next to Nevaeh's.

"Miles is so excited!" Emma told Nevaeh.

"We're all excited, but we're nervous too," Nevaeh said. Suddenly, Emma hugged Nevaeh and started crying.

"Whoa, what's wrong, Emma?" Nevaeh asked.

"Thank you so much," Emma cried.

"What do you mean...thank you?"

Emma stepped back.

"No one in my family ever thought we would see Miles play baseball. We always encouraged him because it was his dream, but we never thought anyone would ever give him a chance. Regardless of, if you win or lose, Miles was a part of a great and loving team. That would never have been possible without you. My entire family is grateful...so...thank you, Nevaeh!"

The day of the single elimination match-up could not have been more beautiful. The sky was crystal clear, with white fluffy clouds. It was 97 degrees, and the birds were chirping. As the stadium filled with spectators, the teams were on the field warming up, or playing catch by their respective dugouts. When the umpires announced that ten minutes remained before play, both teams huddled with their coaches. When Nevaeh made it into the dugout, she saw that Marion Fragnoli and George Hammerhorn had joined them.

"Mrs. Fragnoli and Mr. Hammerhorn will be joining us throughout our journey," Coach Fjord announced. "They are here to lend support, not criticize, so please do not feel nervous. The important thing is to go out there and have fun. Remember, how we react to victory, or defeat will define who we, at Anthem University, are. Be humble, and play the game for love, not greed.

Regardless of if we win or lose, I will forever be grateful to coach this amazing team. Now, hands in."

All at once, the team put their hands into the center of the circle and said, "One, two, three." They lifted their hands to the sky and then yelled, "WOLFPACK!"

Since they were playing at Anthem University, Anthem would field first. The team took their positions on the diamond and waited for the umpire's announcement. Finally, play began with the shout, "PLAY BALL!"

Nevaeh remembered the players from Florida because of their previous encounters. She had a terrific memory and remembered which pitch was each batter's weakness, and which ones they would drill over the fence. Nevaeh and Coach Fjord even worked with the pitchers to develop new signs in case the other teams had stolen their previous signs. In all reality, the signs were the same, but each sign meant a different pitch than it had before. The plan worked perfectly as Kyle retired the first three batters with two strikeouts, and a pop fly to center.

Unfortunately for Anthem's Wolfpack, Ethan Fish and his catcher had also worked out the kinks. Ethan sent Nevaeh down on strikes and proceeded to get a ground ball out, and a pop-up to the first baseman. Coach Fjord had warned the team that this match-up would most likely be a pitcher's duel. The winner would come down to which pitcher got tired first, or which bullpen blew it. As the game continued, neither team got a hit until the top of the seventh inning. Kyle had just thrown a pitch for strike three, but the next batter hit the first pitch back up the center of the diamond for a single. Nevaeh knew that the next batter never swung for power and that he liked low fastballs. She gave the signal to throw an inside fastball, but low. Kyle was an excellent ground ball pitcher and agreed. When the pitch was released, the batter did exactly as Nevaeh expected and hit a ground ball to Allen at second. Allen scooped the ball quickly and threw it to José who was covering second base. Just as quickly as José caught the ball, applying the force play, he threw it to Chadwick at first for the double play.

In the bottom of the seventh inning, Anthem answered with a base hit of their own when Mark Zeti hit a bullet down the first base line. The right fielder for Florida was quick to gather the ball and kept Mark to a single. Kyle hit a pitch directly to Florida's left fielder, and Nevaeh ended an excellent at-bat with a double play. Before Nevaeh hit into the double play, she had worked a full count and fouled five pitches. Although Anthem failed to score, she noticed that Ethan was beginning to look exhausted, as where Kyle still looked fresh. Eventually, the game came down to extra innings. Before the top of the tenth inning started, Coach Fjord checked with both Kyle and Nevaeh before making the decision to leave Kyle in the game.

When the top of the tenth inning started Kyle stepped on the mound once again and dominated. Kyle got two quick outs with two ground balls. When Kyle pitched to Florida's third baseman, everyone held their breath. Kyle needed one more out, and Florida's third baseman was their best hitter. Nevaeh called for a low fastball, and Kyle agreed. When Kyle released the pitch, he also misplaced it. Instead of low, the fastball was high. The batter noticed the mistake, took advantage, and swung.

CRACK!

Nevaeh watched as the ball flew toward the fence in left field. Right as the ball was about to disappear over the fence, Alexander leaped, reached out over the fence, and caught the ball. The crowd at Anthem was louder than thunder. Nevaeh heard the announcer say, "What a spectacular catch by Anthem's left fielder, Alexander Pizza! That might have saved Anthem the game!"

As the bottom of the tenth began, Coach Fjord pulled Kyle from the game and sent Scott Rasp to pinch-hit for him. Scott was a great contact hitter, but slow. Ethan had been pulled from the game, and a scrawny pitcher from their bullpen stood on the mound. Scott hit the first pitch between the center and left fielder. A hit like that would normally be a double, but Scott was a very slow runner. Coach Fjord made the decision to pull Scott out of the game and sent Jacoby Tarly in as a pinch runner. Nevaeh was up to bat next, and Coach Fjord gave her the sign to bunt. The first pitch she saw, she squared her bat and dropped a successful bunt. Jacoby was fast and already at second by the time the ball was fielded, so the third baseman made the decision to throw to first. Nevaeh was fast too, but not fast enough. Nevaeh had hit a successful sacrifice bunt but also issued an out to Anthem. Christopher batted next, and after a long time at bat, he eventually struck out. Brett Swann batted next and didn't miss a beat. Brett swung at the first pitch and lined the ball to left field. Jacoby ran and came around third heading home. The left fielder gathered the ball and fired a bullet to home plate. Jacoby slid headfirst, as the catcher attempted to apply the tag. There was a cloud of dust and silence.

"SAFE!" the umpire yelled as the crowd cheered.

"And Anthem University has just advanced to the semi-finals by a walk-off single!" the announcer exclaimed.

The electricity from the crowd was insane! Before everyone left for the night, Marion Fragnoli and George Hammerhorn shared in the excitement. George ignored Nevaeh, but he announced that the New Jersey Penguins had beaten the Ohio Otters earlier in the day. The new and updated National Championship bracket was:

Anthem Wolfpack?   **New Jersey Penguins**

vs   **Championship**

vs

Paramount Owls?   **New York Elementz**

181

"Anthem's baseball team has not reached the playoffs since Coach Fjord was a player," Marion announced. "Milkshakes are on me at The Moonlit Rose!"

Nevaeh's friends and family arrived at The Moonlit Rose for the celebration and found it overflowing with people. People from all over the community were there to support Nevaeh. Many parents who had children with disabilities, or disabled individuals themselves approached Nevaeh to thank her for giving them the courage to achieve their dreams. She was given thanks for mending a broken system. Many people even thanked Marcus and Marion for allowing such things to happen. Nevaeh later learned that her former English teacher, Mr. Martin had been behind The Moonlit Rose celebration.

"Many of the people you see here have been touched by your actions," Mr. Martin told her. "I always knew you would do great things. I have kept track of you through Coach Fjord, and I received a letter from Miss Saxxby telling me of everything you did for her brother. It only seemed right to honor your hard work and dedication. Also, ya better get used to all the faces here tonight. They're all going to be at your games henceforth cheering your name."

Chapter 24

The morning following the celebration at The Moonlit Rose, Marcus received an email from George Hammerhorn with a subject line that read "Awards".

"Mr. Fjord,

Attached are copies of The National Awards given to Coaches, and players, as well as Anthem's privately given awards to players. Please note that not all directors agree with the decisions of The National Sports Administration. Please share this information with your team. Lastly, it goes without saying that I expect you to continue to make the right choices. ~ G. Hammerhorn

PS. You have not defeated Paramount all year. That is a statistic that MUST change."

Marcus ignored George's demands and opened the attachments.

The following National Awards / Winners are:

Coach of the Year – Marcus Fjord – Anthem

Freshman of the Year – Nevaeh Bennet – Anthem

Pitcher of the Year – Kyle Swabell – Anthem

College Silver Slugger – Robert McGee – Paramount

College Gold Gloves:

(C) - Nevaeh Bennet - Anthem Paramount

(CF) Edward Smith –

(1B) - Gio DeGnaw - Seattle Anthem

(LF) Alexander Pizza –

(2B) - Evan Still - Florida New York Elementz

(RF) Frankie Feliz –

(3B) - Carter Kay – Ohio Otters

(SS) - Brandon Melon – New Jersey Penguins

The following private Awards / Winners are:

Pitcher of the Year – D.J. King

Most Strikeouts – Kyle Swabell

Lowest ERA – Kyle Swabell

Most RBI's - Brett Swann

Highest Average – Christopher Martin

Anthem's Slugger – Chadwick Zomali

Player of the Year – Nevaeh Bennet

Anthem's Golden Glove – Nevaeh Bennet

(New Award) - Most Spirited – Miles Saxxby

Coach Fjord sent the attachments to all the players on the team and posted the lists under the school's sports section on their website. The social media director also posted the lists on all of Anthem's social media. Before long, everyone knew the winners, and the local buzz was on how Anthem took the most awards for the first time in their school's history.

Marcus was required to conduct another interview after the successful win, and the announcement of awards recipients. However, the National Sports Commission granted Marcus a pass due to the looming semi-final match-up against Paramount. The National Sports Commission felt that it was more important for Marcus to conduct practice than answer questions. The only downfall was that Marcus would have to answer double the questions during the next scheduled interview. He did not want to seem ungrateful after winning Coach of the Year, so he agreed. The next interview was scheduled for the day after the conclusion of Anthem vs Paramount. Win or lose, the interview was still taking place.

Paramount had the better record overall, so Anthem had to travel for at least two away games. If game three was needed, it would be contended at Anthem University. The travel time was short, and the team was relieved that they would get to sleep in their own beds. If they advance to the Championship, they will be staying in a hotel for a week.

On the day of the game, Nevaeh was getting off the bus when Kyle ran up to her.

"Look at Robert. I swear he's getting bigger and bigger every time I see him," he said.

Nevaeh laughed. "Well, their mascot is a very large owl."

"Soon enough I'll end up pitching to the owl. If Robert keeps it up, I won't be able to tell them apart," Kyle said laughing.

They both were still laughing as they walked onto the field.

"What's so funny?" Robert demanded.

"Nothing," Nevaeh answered.

"The only funny thing I see here is a one-armed cripple," Robert said laughing.

"You know, it's too bad your Mascot isn't a swine," Kyle said.

Robert looked confused. "Why is that?"

Kyle feigned confusion. "Oh, you didn't know? If your Mascot was a swine, you would be a shoo-in to win the player that looks like their Mascot award."

I won the slugging award, thank you very much!" Robert said defensively.

"Something you didn't deserve," Kyle said. "I'll prove it when I strike you out each time you bat tonight." Robert turned his usual shade of red in frustration.

"Well, at least I have two arms!" he yelled.

Nevaeh just laughed as she walked away. "How pathetic," she thought.

Soon, the game started, and Nevaeh walked to the plate. "The key to beating them is to strike first" she remembered. Ever since Nevaeh hit a home run against Paramount, she had tried to repeat history. This time she had a different plan. The pitch came, and Nevaeh dropped a slow rolling bunt down the first base line. She ran so fast, that her helmet flew off, but she wanted to ensure she would be safe. By the time the ball was fielded and thrown to first, there was no argument about her safety. Nevaeh had beaten the throw by two feet. While Christopher was batting, Robert continued to give the sign to check Nevaeh at first. Nevaeh was too fast, and all the pick-off attempts failed. Nevaeh was planning on stealing with the next pitch. As soon as the ball left the pitcher's fingers, Nevaeh took off. It was that same pitch Christopher hit back up the center and into the outfield for a base hit. Nevaeh rounded third, as the throw was coming home. The ball reached home plate before Nevaeh, but Robert fumbled the ball. Nevaeh slid... "SAFE!" Anthem had an early lead, and Christopher advanced to second on the throw home. Christopher was the next fastest runner and stole third with ease on the next pitch. Brett hit the very next pitch he saw and popped it out into deep center. Once the ball was caught, Christopher tagged up at third and ran home. "Strike early," Nevaeh thought.

Paramount managed to get the next two outs with ease, but Kyle was throwing a gem for Anthem. True to Kyle's word, he struck Robert out at each bat he had. By the seventh inning, all of Paramount remained hitless. Kyle was throwing a perfect game. Anthem had runners in scoring position, but they seemed to be empty threats with each passing inning.

Unfortunately, Kyle's perfect game was blown in the bottom of the ninth inning. Edward Smith hit a double for Paramount. There were no outs, but Robert was hitting next. It was almost as if Robert's appearance at the plate re-motivated them. Robert struck out swinging on three pitches. During the next at-bat, Edward stole third. The distraction was just enough for Kyle. The next pitch Kyle threw was hit to Alexander in shallow left field. As Alexander caught the ball, Edward tagged at third and ran home. Alexander fired the ball home. Nevaeh caught the ball, turned, and leaped to apply the tag. A cloud of dust rose at home plate.

"OUT!" the umpire yelled.

"Anthem's freshman of the year leaps and applies the tag for the final out." the announcer said. "Anthem wins game one with a score of 2 – 0. What a game!"

Chapter 25

"Who else saw the distraught look on Robert's face when Nevaeh tagged Edward out?" José asked as the team ate breakfast the following morning.

"We all saw it," Kyle said. "And we're likely to hear a snort of distress with D.J. on the mound tonight."

"I hear your little sister made a sign of Robert's face and wrote Sir Piggy underneath," D.J. said to Nevaeh.

"She did," Nevaeh admitted, "But I made her rip it up. Remember what Coach said, victories and losses don't define us, but our actions do."

"Robert is an overgrown ass though," Chadwick said.

"Yes," Nevaeh agrees, "But let his actions define him. We should stay humble like Coach said."

It took a while, but eventually, the team came around and agreed not to pick on Robert. "I agree he deserves it, but we shouldn't stoop to that level," was Nevaeh's big sticking point.

Game two of the semi-finals would be an afternoon game to allow for travel if game three was needed. Coach Fjord extended an invitation for former Coach Kozlowski to join them in the dugout. Marion and George were already joining them, so what damage could one more person bring? Coach Fjord had also given the team over to the new Athletic Trainer, Jordan Heart for a few hours in order to work on their pre-game stretches. Jordan knew how to work their muscles just enough to rid them of pain and leave them limber to reduce injury.

As the second game approached, the stadium began to fill with spectators. Nevaeh was walking with Miles when Miles pointed out Emma in the stands. Nevaeh not only saw Emma, but she saw her parents, grandparents, Vinny, Rachel, Keven, and Morgan waving at her. Morgan even brought Halo.

"She brings that dog everywhere," Nevaeh told Miles.

Before they knew it, the umpire was yelling "TEN MINUTES UNTIL THE START OF THE GAME." Everyone huddled in the dugout, and George told them to win.

"We just need to win," George demanded..." no game three."

Coach Fjord and the team had grown used to George's relentless demands and simply ignored him.

"Do you hear me?" George yelled.

"Yeah, yeah," Mark said waving his hand. "The entire stadium hears your bellowing."

Suddenly the team heard "PLAY BALL!" and got into their batting lineup. Nevaeh led and tried to strike early, but Robert readjusted the pitches with the pitchers. She hit the ball but lined it directly into the second baseman's glove. Christopher and Brett suffered similar outcomes, and soon D.J. King was on the mound pitching for Anthem. Any spectator would have been able to tell that D.J. was nervous. D.J. was so nervous that he couldn't find the plate and walked the first three batters, which loaded the bases for Robert. Nevaeh called a time-out and ran to the pitching mound to talk to D.J. They only had a limited time to talk, so Nevaeh did her best to calm D.J. down. Nevaeh returned to her position behind home plate and gave the signal for the first pitch. D.J. looked more confident with these pitches, but Robert won the slugging award for a reason and hit a grand slam. After the grand slam, Coach Fjord called a time-out and spoke with both D.J. and Nevaeh. Coach Fjord's pep talk worked as D.J. sent the next three batters down in order. When Nevaeh returned to the dugout, George attacked her in a fury.

"What are you doing out there?" he demanded.

"Um, I'm playing baseball?" she replied, confused.

"No, you're calling pitches that benefit Paramount. If you don't care about winning a championship, you can stay on the bench!" George declared.

"Winning isn't everything, sir," Nevaeh answered curtly. "And for the record, I'm trying my hardest."

"Well, you better start trying harder if you want to stay on the team!"

"Sir, it's my fault, not Nevaeh's," D.J. interjected. "I'm just really nervous," D.J. added.

George looked at D.J. in a fury.

"Don't you ever interrupt me, boy!" George snapped.

At this point, Marcus was walking over to see what all the yelling was about. George was still speaking to D.J.

"And don't you ever take the blame for a female's blunder? And one other thing, if you wish to stay on the team, you better find your confidence, ALSO..."

"I'm sorry..." Marcus interrupted. "I seem to have been misinformed. When exactly was I removed as head coach?"

"You haven't been removed...YET!" George blurted back at Marcus.

"Then let me handle the coaching," Marcus said sternly. "If you want to win a championship so badly, sit on that bench and keep your mouth shut!" George was shocked but trotted to the bench anyway.

"Don't let Mr. Hammerhorn lower your morale. You're doing great. This is a tough team to play," Coach Fjord said to Nevaeh and D.J.

There was not a lot of room for a pep talk, as the Paramount pitcher retired the side in order. Nevaeh grabbed her gear and took her position behind home plate once more.

As the half-inning began, D.J. was throwing his pitches better, but Nevaeh could tell that he was still nervous. The inning seemed to go better as D.J. got the first two batters out via pop-ups. The lineup flipped back, and D.J. found himself facing the top of the order once again, and it was only the bottom of the second. Although D.J.'s pitches were better, he gave up three consecutive singles to load the bases for Robert once more. Nevaeh was bound and determined to deny Robert another grand slam. She gave the signal for the slider away. D.J. agreed and threw the pitch. Robert swung and missed.

"STRIKE ONE!"

Next, Nevaeh gave the signal for a low change-up. D.J. agreed and threw the ball. Robert swung and hit the ball to Allen at second base. Allen scooped the ball to throw to first but fumbled. All runners were safe, and another run came across home plate to score. Anthem was down by five runs.

"And that's scored as an E4," the announcer stated.

The only plus to Allen's error was that the run did not count as an RBI for Robert. As Nevaeh was thinking about what pitch to call, she looked over at Robert and remembered how he attempted to pick her off several times in the game before.

"He's got a decent lead on first..." she thought. "And he's slow."

She made the decision and gave the signal for D.J. to throw to first. D.J. agreed. Chadwick also noticed the signal and moved slowly to the bag so Robert wouldn't notice. As quick as a snake, D.J. turned and threw to first. Robert tried to dive back to first, but Chadwick caught the ball and applied the tag.

"OUT!" The umpire yelled.

"What a tremendous pick-off at first to end the inning!" the announcer shouted.

The top of the third saw Mark Zeti leading off for Anthem. Like the first six before him, Mark failed to hit as he hit a pop-up to the third baseman. José batted next and gave the anthem their first hit with a single to center field. D.J. batted next and hit a double. The ball split the center and right fielder.

"He must be getting tired," Nevaeh thought.

When Nevaeh came to the plate, Anthem had one out, and two runners in scoring position. The first pitch thrown was a change-up, and Nevaeh dropped a perfectly placed bunt down the first base line. José saw the sign from Coach Fjord and started running before she even made contact. José crossed home plate with ease, and Nevaeh was too fast to be thrown out. The suicide squeeze play was successful! Nevaeh ran on the next pitch and successfully stole second. Anthem once again had two runners in scoring position, and with Nevaeh's speed, all they needed was a single to score both. Christopher did exactly what Anthem needed...a lined base hit to right. D.J. and Nevaeh both scored, but Christopher was thrown out at second, trying to stretch the hit into a double. Brett Swann batted next and struck out swinging. The score was 5 – 3 in Paramount's favor.

In the bottom of the third, D.J. finally found his confidence and retired the side in order. Paramount's Coach pulled their starter and sent in a new pitcher who dominated Anthem for most of the game. D.J. continued to answer, and the innings remained scoreless until the top of the ninth. In the top of the ninth, Chadwick hit a solo home run, to put Anthem one run away from tying the game. Anthem had two outs, and Allen Redwood came to the plate. Paramount's coach made the decision to pull their reliever and bring in their closing pitcher. On the second pitch of the at-bat, Allen lined a ground ball to the shortstop, who threw to first for the final out. Paramount had won game two and tied the series 1 – 1. Game three, and the final game of the semi-finals would be the following night at Anthem's home field.

As the team rode home to Anthem University, Coach Fjord made the following announcement.

"I have just received an email letting me know that the New York Elementz swept the New Jersey Penguins and are awaiting the outcome of tomorrow night's game to see who they will face for The National Championships. As you know, the New York Elementz has won The National Championships for the last seven consecutive years. They are seeking their eighth straight. We have the opportunity to not only make history once, but twice. After we win tomorrow night, not only will we advance to the finals for the first time, but we will de-throne one of the best teams to ever play college baseball and bring Anthem their first National title."

Everyone cheered, but Nevaeh thought, "If we win tomorrow, our biggest challenge still awaits us."

Chapter 26

As Nevaeh sat in the locker room before game three, she could hear the spectators filing in.

"Who is going to be my pitcher tonight?" Nevaeh asked her coach.

"Phillip VanSnow," Marcus answered. We need Kyle rested if we advance."

"Sounds good," Nevaeh replied. "Have you ever been so nervous you felt like throwing up?" she asked.

"It's funny you say that," Marcus said. "Twenty years ago, I sat on this very bench, feeling the exact same way. It was Anthem's first-ever wild card elimination. I was more nervous than you would believe. Coach Kozlowski and your dad helped calm me, but I was still nervous when I went to the mound. Your dad though, if he was nervous, he didn't show it. He was like a rock. After my injury, your dad was acting Captain. We lost the semifinals, but your dad gave us one hell of a fight. You are just like him. Determined. You have heart."

"Yeah, but you were really good too. My dad failed at calling the right pitches after your injury. What if I do too?" Nevaeh asked Marcus.

"Your dad did not fail to call the right pitches. The pitchers failed to throw them. I made mistakes where I shook off his suggestions and gave up homers. Once I started listening to him, I started breaking records. The most important position is a catcher. They see the entire field and know the opposing batters better than any pitcher. You have your father's blood, and you have him in your heart. I've already instructed all of our pitchers to trust your judgment. They won't be shaking off any of your suggestions. This game and The National Championship are yours to win. You have already shattered barriers, and I have faith in you."

"Thank you, coach, but I ..."

"No buts," Marcus interrupted. You are what this school and this team needed. Heck, you're what this sport needed. Your father could tell you to stop doubting yourself. This game and this championship series are not important. What's important is that you become the player you're supposed to be, and the player you're meant to be is a leader. One who could potentially lead the team to their first championship. The choice is yours. Doubt yourself and move on with life or be your father's daughter." Marcus turned and left Nevaeh sitting on the bench. She thought about what her coach had said, grabbed her locket, and looked at the picture.

"I *AM* my father's daughter!" she said as she walked onto the diamond, and she saw signs all around the stadium in support of her. Some signs were simple and said, "Nevaeh #4," while others mentioned inclusion and breaking barriers. A group of people held a banner over the outfield wall that said, "Nevaeh Bennet #4, making the world better one catch at a time!" The biggest surprise for Nevaeh was that some people had made huge cardboard cutouts of her head. "Mr. Martin didn't lie when he said I would have support," she thought.

As the game began and Nevaeh took her place behind home plate, the crowd erupted! Nevaeh remembered what Coach Fjord said, and methodically made the calls for pitches. Nevaeh's calls worked in Anthem's favor as Phillip retired the side in order. As the inning switched from top to bottom, the crowd started chanting, "Nevaeh! Nevaeh!" as she approached the plate. With her bat in hand, she looked out to the crowd and felt their support. Her friends and family were behind home plate, and Morgan not only had Halo, but she too had a huge cut out of her sister's head. Nevaeh swung on the first pitch and hit a ball that divided the outfielders. The crowd cheered so loud that Nevaeh thought her eardrums would burst. Nevaeh looked and determined that she was fast enough to turn the double into a triple. As she rounded a second, the crowd got louder. She slid into third as the ball was being thrown in.

"SAFE!" the umpire yelled.

The next at-bat, Christopher Martin hit a pop-up to the centerfielder, which should have been caught, but the wind took the ball at the last second and hit the grass. Nevaeh scored easily. When she got back to the dugout, she told the team that they needed to take advantage of that error and strike first. The team did exactly that and batted around the order. Nevaeh had two at bat in the first and Anthem scored seven runs before Paramount finally got them out. Phillip and Nevaeh continued to dominate the opposing team, and Paramount had to go to their bullpen early. By the time the ninth inning came, Anthem had a commanding lead of 16 – 0. Every time Anthem scored, the players on Paramount became careless, especially Robert. All of Paramount's players were desperate for a rally and refused to play small ball.

"They're unfocused," Nevaeh told Phillip. "Throw high fastballs and they're going to swing hoping to send one over the fence."

"And if they hit one over?" Phillip asked.

"We have a big enough lead," Nevaeh said as she shrugged.

Paramount never hit any over the fence, and Nevaeh's prediction turned out to be correct. Every batter swung at the fastballs hoping to be their team's hero.

The closest that Paramount came to a rally was in the top of the ninth inning. With two outs, Paramount's third baseman hit a bloop single. Robert came to the plate next, giving Nevaeh the stink eye the entire time. She gave the signal for the high fastball, and Phillip agreed. Phillip threw the pitch, but the pitch was slightly lower than Nevaeh wanted. Robert swung and hit the ball deep to center field. Brett ran back as far as he could, noticed the warning track approaching, and leaped halfway up the wall. He used his momentum and pushed with his feet. Brett reached as high as he possibly could and caught the ball. Brett fell back onto the warning track, rolled, and stood showing everyone the ball. Brett had not only robbed Robert of a home run but of his championship dreams as well.

The crowd was electric as the team huddled together on the pitching mound. When Coach Fjord joined the celebration, Jordan and a few other players grabbed the cooler of water and dumped it onto the players. For the first time in Anthem's history, they would be competing for The National Championship.

The finalized National bracket was as follows:

South Division
North Division

Anthem Wolfpack   **vs**
New York Elementz

Anthem was clearly the underdog, but they had momentum and heart. Meanwhile, Robert beat the ground with his bat out of frustration, as Anthem celebrated! Nevaeh noticed

Robert and thought, "How you handle defeat, defines who you are. That says a lot."

Chapter 27

With the completion of the semifinals and Anthem's successful advancement, Marcus had to endure another interview session. As much as he despised the interviews, he was a man of his word and consented. Marcus had grown accustomed to the routine and instantly said, "Please, one at a time" as he entered the conference room at Anthem University. When he reached the podium, he heard the first question.

"Anthem players won quite a few awards, what is your take on that?"

"I believe the students who won those awards deserved them. They worked hard, and I couldn't be prouder of them," Marcus replied.

"And what about your win as Coach of the Year?"

"For that, I am very appreciative. I was shocked, and still am. Overall, I'm very thankful for the honor," Marcus answered.

"Obviously, you're pleased with your team's performance, but what are your feelings on advancing to the finals for the first time, and what is your plan going forth?"

Marcus smiled. "If I told you my plans, then that would ruin them. As to my feelings, I think it is safe to say that the entire team and I are excited to go somewhere we have never been.

Regardless of the outcome, we will be forever grateful to have had the journey."

"Does it frustrate you to be called the underdogs?"

"Why would that frustrate me? It's obvious that we're the underdogs. When you looked at the match-up on paper, we weren't even supposed to defeat Paramount. Now we face our undefeated team and the winner of the last seven National Championships. Of course, we're the underdogs," Marcus replied.

"With the injury Howard Coff sustained, we saw you place D.J. King into the second position in the rotation. Can we expect another rotation change after Mr. King's poor performance?"

"D.J. King did not perform 'poorly,'" Marcus said as he placed air quotes around the word poorly. "He simply had a few minor setbacks. Nerves played a part as it was his first major game as a starter. However, yes, the rotation will be modified for the championship.

"May we ask what this new rotation looks like?"

"The rotation will remain similar to the original. Kyle Swabell is our ace, Phillip VanSnow is second, Garth Silinski is third, and D.J. will be our fourth starter. As always, Keith Elia is our closing pitcher."

Marcus glanced at his watch and said, "With all due respect, I really must be going. I have a practice to attend before we travel."

With that, Marcus exited the conference room and felt positive for once doing so. "This interview session actually went well," Marcus thought as he exited through the double oak doors.

Chapter 28

The team would have a week to rest before the start of The National Championship. They traveled early and arrived in South Carolina six days before game one. Coach Fjord took the opportunity to go over the footage of The New York Elementz's previous games. They also reviewed footage of the last seven National titles to look for consistencies or weaknesses. The first thing that Nevaeh and Coach Fjord noticed was that The Elementz only used a three-pitcher rotation, whereas Anthem used four. The Elementz rotation consisted of their ace Jack Wayne who was a Senior, another Senior, Bradley Kearns, and a Junior named Michael Rotriff. The second thing they noticed was the Elementz record. They had zero losses on the season, and their playoff record was perfect as well.

The more that Nevaeh analyzed the footage, the more flaws she found. She shared what she observed with her team hoping it would lead them to victory.

"You better get used to this," Coach Fjord told her.

"Why is that?" she asked.

"Because you're going to be the team captain next year," he told her.

"But Kyle's the captain," she said.

"He's also a Senior," Coach Fjord replied laughing.

"Oh, yeah. I forgot," Nevaeh said as she laughed back.

Over the next couple of days, Coach Fjord, and Jordan Heart worked diligently with the team. They continued to practice, stretch, and review footage, looking for flaws. Time flew, and game one quickly approached. The stadium was larger than any stadium Anthem had previously played in. Nonetheless, the stadium filled every seat with spectators. The stadium was split evenly between Anthem supporters and New York Elementz supporters. All around the stadium, banners and flags were displayed that read "College World Series National Championship" or "New York Elementz vs Anthem Wolfpack." As spectators were entering the stadium, they were given souvenir booklets that contained pictures of the members on each team, and their statistics. Prior to the start of the game, they could find both team's mascots walking around the crowd. The Wolf for Anthem, and the Hurricane for New York.

Finally, the President of The National Sports Commission walked to the microphone near the pitching mound. The crowd grew silent.

"Good afternoon, ladies and gentlemen. My name is Montgomery Baxter, and I am pleased to welcome you to the two-hundred-and-fourth College World Series. This year's series will feature the New York defending champions for the last seven years facing the underdogs from Texas. With a season record of

50 – 0, we have The New York Elementz. From the South Division, with an overall record of 39 – 11, we have The Anthem Wolfpack. Before we begin to play, I want to remind spectators that we encourage you to get loud. Cheer with your heart's desire. However, please keep in mind that The National Sports Commission has a zero-tolerance policy for poor sportsmanship, and our security will remove you, if necessary. Overall, enjoyed the game. Stay safe and have fun!"

At the conclusion of The National Sports Commission's President's speech, The National Anthem was performed by a local choir. And to the surprise, and awe, of everyone, including Rachel and Nevaeh's family, Keven signed the beautiful Anthem, perfectly and proudly. Everyone was standing, with their hands over their hearts, or saluting, with tears in their eyes. Applause and cheers thundered throughout the stadium as the National Anthem's last note finished. Keven bowed graciously and blew a kiss to Rachel in the stands. As the audience began to sit down, the announcer roared...

"PLAY BALL!"

Anthem won the coin toss to determine which team would have a "home" field advantage. Even though Anthem was playing in South Carolina, all home-field advantage meant was that they would bat in the bottom of the innings giving them an opportunity for a walk-off. Each game hereafter would alternate. This means that the "home" field advantage would go to New York in game two, back to Anthem in game three, and so on.

Nevaeh took her position behind home plate and waited for the batter. She only knew the opposing pitchers' names and referred to the batters by the number on their jerseys. The numbers are also how she remembered their strengths and weaknesses. Nevaeh studied tapes of New York's games with Coach Fjord, and when she was alone in her hotel room.

When number seven stepped out of the dugout, she instantly knew him as the "free swinger." Because of his lack of discipline at the plate, Nevaeh called for pitches out of the strike zone. Kyle listened to her suggestions and sent number seven back to the dugout after three pitches. The other two outs came just as easily, and quick as that, the top of the first was over, and the Wolfpack was coming to bat.

New York's ace Jack Wayne was the chosen pitcher for game one, and Anthem soon learned why he was their ace. Jack sent Nevaeh and Christopher down on strikes. Brett hit the ball, but New York was there to catch it.

"It's almost like they're wizards," Nevaeh told her Coach.

"No," Marcus replied. "Just incredibly talented."

Nevaeh and Kyle gave New York a run for their money, however.

Kyle and Nevaeh had a perfect routine. Nevaeh kept switching pitches, and neither team allowed a hit until the eighth inning. New York managed to strike and hit back-to-back singles. Number seventeen was hitting next for New York, and Nevaeh gave the signal for a low two-seam fastball. The plan was to go for a double play since the runner on second was one of New York's slowest. They would deal with the next batter, and hopefully, New York would fail to get a run across. Number seventeen had a different idea and attempted a sacrifice bunt to advance both runners. The bunted ball did not travel far from home plate and Nevaeh reacted quickly, threw off her glove, grabbed the ball, and fired to third. Mark tagged third and fired to Allen at second, who quickly fired to Chadwick at first.

"What a terrific play!" the announcer shouted. "A rare two, six, four, three triple play to end the inning! Absolutely outstanding!"

In the bottom of the eighth inning, Chadwick ruined New York's perfect game when he blasted a deep solo home run over the center field fence. After Chadwick's homerun, New York's Coach pulled Jack from the game and replaced him with their closer. The closing pitcher for New York did his job perfectly, giving up a ground rule double, then proceeded to record the final outs. However, the damage had been done. Coach Fjord made the decision to pull Kyle from the game as well and gave Keith an opportunity for the save. Nevaeh spent a lot of time with all her pitchers and gave Keith a quick rundown. Keith performed as expected, and Anthem took a game-one victory, with a score of 1 – 0.

Chapter 29

The New York Elementz was a great team, and with all great teams, they adapted and grew from their prior mistakes. New York dominated in game two, in what would be better recognized as a slaughter. Nevaeh had attempted to change pitches and location, but it all proved helpless. New York won game two with a score of 27 – 0. The night of game three shared a very similar outcome as game two. The only difference was that New York was not able to score as high, and Anthem got onto the scoreboard. New York won game three with a score of 17 – 3. One of Anthem's three points was from a bases-loaded balk, and Anthem really only earned two runs that game.

"New York leads the series 2 – 1. Every game henceforth is an elimination game for us," Coach Fjord told his team.

"I'm telling you, they're using some sort of witchcraft and wizardry," Nevaeh said. "They're hitting every pitch."

"Maybe they're using magnets?" José asked.

Coach Fjord laughed. "I think our pitchers would notice magnets on the balls. As to Nevaeh's witchcraft and wizardry idea, I can't say for certain, but it's highly unlikely. We knew from the start that this was going to be our biggest challenge yet. Some critics even say that we don't belong here. We may be on the brink of elimination, but we need to remind ourselves that we have something that no one else does, and that's heart."

D.J. stood abruptly and said, "We can't lose. For years I was told that I was too short to play baseball at the collegiate level. I worked hard and proved all those naysayers and critics wrong. Coach Fjord gave me an opportunity to play, and he helped show me that it was what was in my heart that mattered. We all have heart. Look at Nevaeh. She has the biggest heart of all of us. She's worked harder than any of us and has been supportive when we have been down. Tonight's game isn't about winning, but we're going to. Personally, I'm going to dig deep into my heart and play to the best ability. I hope you all do the same."

"Very nicely said," Marcus replied. "Now let's get out there and show them that we are no underdogs. We're the Wolfpack, and they're our prey."

D.J.'s motivational speech about the heart may have been exactly what Anthem needed to bring them back to life. In the top of the first inning, Nevaeh hit a solo home run to the short porch in the right field, but that was not all. Christopher and Brett managed base hits, and Chadwick drilled a ball over the left-field fence. The early assault gave Anthem a 4 – 0 lead. As the bottom of the first came. D.J. kept to his word and dominated the side. Nevaeh had made mention of the fire she saw in D.J.'s eyes and how he had never seemed so determined.

Because of New York's three-man pitching rotation, Jack Wayne was on the mound for New York. Jack was already furious that he lost game one, and Anthem's early lead only made him angrier.

"I can't believe I gave up a home run to a girl!" Nevaeh heard him yell as she rounded the bases in the first. After the early attack by Anthem, game four became a pitcher's duel. Jack found his determination and refused to allow a base runner. D.J. was doing the same, but Nevaeh could see he was getting tired. D.J. gave up a hit here and there, but he never allowed them to score.

Before the bottom of the eighth inning, Nevaeh urged her coach to pull D.J. from the game. "He's tired," she said. "Plus, he's a reliever. He's not used to pitching a full game."

Coach Fjord disagreed and kept D.J. in the game ignoring Nevaeh's pleas. When the bottom of the eighth started, Anthem had a lead of 4 – 0. However, by the end of the eighth, the game would be tied 4 – 4. When D.J. stepped onto the mound for the eighth time that night, he looked exhausted. He gave up two back-to-back signals, which placed a runner on first and second. D.J. managed to get a strikeout next but gave up an RBI double with the next batter, and a three-run homerun with the batter after that. After the three-run blast, D.J. found enough gasoline to reignite the fire in his eyes, but only long enough to get the remaining two outs. When the team sat in the dugout between innings, D.J. told everyone he was sorry, and asked Coach to take him out of the game.

Jack was still pitching like a machine. In the top of the ninth inning, Jack sent José back to the dugout on strikes. Coach Fjord agreed to pull D.J. from the game and sent Reggie Botary to the plate as a pinch hitter. Reggie fouled off a few pitches but struck out. Nevaeh went to the plate next, but before doing so, she grabbed her locket, closed her eyes, and thought of her father. When she reached the plate, she could see the determination in Jack's eyes. Jack was not about to give Nevaeh a chance for another home run.

"Just look and wait for one mistake," Nevaeh thought. After ten pitches, she started to wonder if a mistake would come. She had two balls and two strikes, and she had to keep fouling off pitches. The next pitch Jack threw, Nevaeh hit for a foul ball. Finally, Nevaeh caught a break, and the next pitch was ball three. She fouled off the next two pitches. As Nevaeh raised her bat and awaited the next pitch, she observed a flash of doubt as Jack shook off his catcher.

"He's disagreeing with the catcher," she thought. "here's the mistake."

She could feel the sweat dripping down her face as Jack found his footing, wound up, and released a fastball over the center of home plate. "The mistake," she thought. Nevaeh closed her eyes as she swung and heard the wood of the bat meet the ball.

CRACK!

She opened her eyes and started running towards first, as fast as she could. The right fielder was on the run, and she listened to the announcer.

"The right fielder is on the chase. He's at the warning track. The wall. He leaps, but it's out of reach. Anthem's freshman catcher hits her second home run of the game and Anthem takes the lead by one!"

As Nevaeh rounded third, her teammates met her at home plate. High fives were passed around, and Nevaeh heard the cheers from the crowd as cutouts of her face waved back and forth.

Jack got Christopher out on a first-pitch groundball, and Nevaeh returned to home plate with her gear. Keith was summoned from the bullpen to close out the game and earn a save. The first two batters went down with ease, but the third batter was Jack. Nevaeh noticed that he still had the look of determination in his eyes, but the frustration had returned as well. Jack at bat was like Nevaeh's as he kept fouling the pitches off. After the thirteenth pitch of the at-bat, Nevaeh thought, "How can I use his frustration against him?" After a few seconds of thought, she had her risky answer. "Jack's frustration might compel him to swing through a high fastball...but if Keith's aim is off, it could tie the game," she thought.

Nevaeh decided to take the risk and gave the sign for a high fastball. Keith nodded in agreement and delivered the pitch. When Jack saw the high fastball, his eyes grew open wide. Jack swung and brushed the bottom of the ball with the bat. Nevaeh caught it in her glove, heard the snap of leather, and ...

"STRIKE THREE!"

Anthem fans were cheering, and started to jump up and down, cheering to their heart's content! As the announcer's voice rang throughout the stadium.

"Anthem ties up the series after a successful risk by their young catcher. These wolves mean business!"

Chapter 30

"New York's three-man rotation may very well work in our favor," Coach Fjord told his team before the start of game five. "Their rotation forced them to use their ace yesterday, and because of our four-man rotation, our ace is well-rested and ready to go."

The members of the Anthem Wolfpack knew that despite all their hard work, tonight's game could go either way. They were well aware that New York had been surprised twice by the Wolfpack and that they would do everything necessary to stop a third surprise. They also knew that like them, New York would adjust to the weakness and make the needed changes. If Anthem were to win The National Championship, it would not be easy. Nevaeh and Kyle talked for hours about different strategies, and pitch orders. Coach Fjord went over hours of footage showing how New York's Bradley Kearns changes his pitch selection with each game, and Jordan spent hours meditating and stretching with the players.

Three hours before the start of the game, Nevaeh received a text from Morgan. The text contained a photo of Morgan, Vinny, Rachel, and Halo and the caption read, "Good Luck tonight, Sis! We love you and can't wait to see you hold the trophy." Nevaeh appreciated the text and welcomed the winning encouragements.

Before the start of the final game, the team gathered with Coach Fjord, former Coach Kozlowski, Marion Fragnoli, and George Hammerhorn.

"Tonight's game will be our toughest yet," Coach Fjord began. "Win or lose, you are all Champions. At our very first practice, I told you all the wins, and Championships do not define who we are, but rather *how* we handle such wins or losses define us. When I was your age, all I wanted to do was win. I learned that message from Coach Kozlowski, and it took me years to understand it. My injury was my sign to be humble and handle things with dignity. All of you have learned that message early and are champions in your own right. When you walk out onto that diamond and see signs with your name on them in the crowd, that means you're doing something right. Especially you, Nevaeh. This team has jumped over barriers and shattered glass ceilings all year long. A lot of that has been credited to ME, but the credit belongs to Nevaeh and the rest of this team who have supported her in making Anthem University inclusive. We don't need a Championship to be the best. This team has heart, determination, and love for the sport and one another. I know that New York will bring their Game tonight, but so will you. Win or lose, I couldn't have asked for a better team!"

After the singing of the National Anthem with the choir and Keven signing, game five started, and Anthem University was awarded a "home" field advantage as carried over from the game one-coin toss. Nevaeh took her place behind home plate, and the game began. As expected, New York made modifications and changed their batting line-up. Number two was hitting first and lined the first pitch back up the center. New York took a lesson from Coach Fjord and attempted to strike, early, but Nevaeh and Kyle saw through it. Number two took off running on Kyles's next pitch, but Nevaeh called for a high fastball. Nevaeh caught the ball, threw it up, dropped her glove, and fired a bullet to second.

"OUT!"

Kyle and Nevaeh managed to get a strikeout and pop up to end the inning after the attempted steal.

Nevaeh started the game in a similar manner when she hit a line drive to left field for a base hit off Bradley Kearns. Unlike number two, she successfully stole second on the next pitch but was picked off when Christopher hit a liner straight into the second baseman's glove. The play happened so quickly that Nevaeh did not have enough time to slide back into the bag. Bradley got the next out with ease, and before long, Nevaeh was back behind the plate, and Kyle was on the pitching mound.

The next five innings continued to mirror each other. Kyle had given up back-to-back doubles before obtaining the three outs, which allowed one run to cross the plate in one-half inning, and Anthem answered in the next with a solo home run. This continued until the seventh inning when New York failed to score. With two innings remaining, and the game tied 5 – 5, this was Anthem's chance to take their first lead of the game. New York pulled Bradley from the game and replaced him with their third starter, Michael Rotriff. Michael entered the game fully refreshed and sent the side down in order. The eighth inning went exactly as the seventh, and both teams found themselves in a score-or-lose situation as they entered the ninth.

"How are you feeling?" Coach Fjord asked Kyle.

"Great, Coach," Kyle responded.

"Do you think you can handle the ninth, or should I send Keith in?" Coach asked.

"I've got one more inning in me," Kyle told him.

Marcus looked at Nevaeh, and she agreed with Kyle. Coach Fjord sent Kyle back to the mound for one last inning.

At the start of the ninth inning, Kyle obtained the first two outs with ease. He walked the next batter, and the batter after that hit a base hit that allowed the runner on first to advance to third, leaving runners on the corners with two outs. Nevaeh was methodically calling pitches hoping for a strike when she noticed the runner at first edging toward second. She called for a pitch outside. Kyle agreed and threw. Once he threw the ball, the runner on first took off for second. Nevaeh caught the ball, dropped her glove, and threw to second. At that same moment, she realized the runner on third was stealing home. The umpire at second yelled "SAFE!", and Allen fired the ball back towards Nevaeh. All of this happened so fast that Nevaeh never had time to get her glove back on. She caught the ball barehanded, kept a grip through the pain, and leaped back toward home plate to apply the tag!

"Please be on time," she thought.

As the dust settled at home, everyone sat in silence awaiting the verdict.

"OUT!" the umpire yelled.

Cheers from Anthem's fans were booming through the stadium as the teams switched sides.

The bottom of the ninth inning was led off by Anthem's second baseman, Allen Redwood. Allen worked a full count and earned a base on balls after he fouled a few pitches off. The winning run was on first. Alexander batted next and worked another walk. New York called a time-out, and shortly after, the coach pulled Michael from the game and sent their closing pitcher to the mound. Their closing pitcher was well rested as he struck both Mark and José out. With two outs and runners on first and second, Kyle approached the plate. Kyle was determined to give his team a walk of victory and stood eyeing the pitcher. As the pitch came towards Kyle, he lifted his foot and prepared to swing. At the last moment, Kyle realized that the pitch was thrown inside and was about to hit him. Kyle pulled back, but not far enough. The pitch hit Kyle in the elbow. Just like that, it was up to Nevaeh to be the hero and hit a walk-off.

"Okay, Nevaeh. This is the moment you have waited for!" Coach Fjord said.

Nevaeh grabbed her bat and walked to the steps of the dugout. When she investigated the crowd, she saw her family. She saw Morgan, her mother, her grandparents, and even Halo. She saw Rachel and Vinny. They all stood holding signs and cheering for Nevaeh. Then Nevaeh noticed Emma and her family holding similar signs and cheering for Miles. Nevaeh looked back at Miles on the bench, stepped back off the step, and turned to her coach.

"No, Coach. This is the moment that Miles has waited for." Coach Fjord looked confused.

"You're aware that the game is tied 5 – 5?" he asked.

"Yes, sir."

"And you're aware that this is the Championship game?"

"Yes."

"And that we have two outs? This could very well be our only chance to win the title."

"Yes, sir," Nevaeh said. "I understand all of that, but Miles and his family have waited for this opportunity as well."

"What the bloody hell is going on here?" George demanded.

"Miss Bennet would like me to send Mr. Saxxby to the plate in her stead," Marcus replied.

"Has your bloody cripple lost her mind?" George yelled. "She should be thankful to have the opportunity to win the game, and she wants to throw it all away for some retard?"

Nevaeh had heard enough and screamed at George.

"How dare you use words like that! Ever since I met you, I thought you were concerned about the school, but now I see that you're just a grumpy old man!"

"You watch how you speak to me, or you'll be finding a new college to attend next semester!" George said. "Now, grab your bat and win me my Championship!"

"This entire season, you didn't want me to play, and now you do?" Nevaeh asked. "Coach, I'm sorry, but you can do the right thing and put Miles in or put someone else in because I'm sitting out!"

"If she won't bat, then put Xander in," George demanded. "Be the coach you claim to be and win the Championship!"

Marcus looked at Nevaeh, then to George, and out at the fans. He took a step towards Xander but stopped when Nevaeh said, "You told everyone that winning meant nothing. You said that our actions and how we handle situations define us. Was all that a lie? You claim that coach Kozlowski taught you that, but did you ever really learn? You, yourself talked about how this team had broken barriers and already won. You're the coach, and you make the decision, but I would rather have been on the team that gave the boy with Down's Syndrome a moment to live his dream, rather than be on the team that denied an opportunity and won. When you selected me as your starting catcher, you said that everyone deserved a chance to play. Miles sits on that bench every day wishing he could play but never gets the chance. His family sits in that crowd every day and chants his name knowing he will never get the chance to play. You told me that I was creating my own legacy, but I would rather have nothing, and give someone else a chance. Coach, I ask you to please put your own legacy behind you as well and do the right thing. Would you rather be known as the coach that won Anthem their first National title or the coach that gave an opportunity to a boy to fulfill his childhood dreams when no one else would? A wise man once told me that your actions define who you are. Well coach, tonight, your actions will define you and your legacy."

When Nevaeh was done, she was emotional, and she had tears rolling down her cheeks. She walked away and sat next to Miles on the bench.

"You better make the right decision, Marcus," George said as he pushed his finger into Marcus' shoulder. "Your job might very well depend on it."

George walked away and left Marcus with Marion.

225

"What's your decision going to be?" the umpire asked. We have a game to finish."

Marcus looked at Marion, and Marion said..." You're the coach, Marcus. It's your choice, but I remember what you said when we reviewed Nevaeh's application. Do you?"

"No, what?" Marcus asked.

"You might do well to learn something from that young lady," Marion said as she walked away.

"Clock's ticking! What's going on?" the umpire asked.

"We're sending a pinch hitter to the plate." Marcus turned towards the bench. "Saxxby, grab your bat."

Chapter 31

Miles couldn't believe what he had just heard. His eyes were as wide as saucers. "ME?" he said.

"That's right!" Coach Fjord said as he handed him his helmet and bat. Nevaeh sat and listened to the announcer.

"In an unprecedented move, Coach Fjord has elected to send a pinch hitter to the plate instead of Nevaeh Bennet."

Nevaeh waited for the announcer to say Miles's name and looked at Emma once he did. Emma and her parents broke down in tears. "They never thought they would see this moment," Nevaeh thought.

As Miles approached the plate, the crowd fell silent. When Miles swung and missed at the first pitch, the jeers started flowing from New York fans.

"You better kiss that championship goodbye," one fan yelled.

"Special Ed here won't make contact," yelled another.

"Your coach just handed New York a win," was one more rude comment.

When Miles swung and missed at the next pitch, Morgan was quick to yell encouragement.

"You can do it, Miles!" Morgan yelled.

"Believe in yourself!" Emma yelled.

"You've got this Bud!" Vinny yelled.

Nevaeh knew that New York's pitcher thought Miles would be an easy out, so she joined her voice to the encouraging yells.

"Remember how we practiced! Keep your eye on the ball!" she yelled out.

Meanwhile, George was throwing a fit inside the dugout. Miles heard Nevaeh and did exactly as she said and kept his eye on the ball. As the pitch came, Miles stood still.

"BALL!" yelled the umpire.

By now, the encouraging yells were drowning out the rude ones. Some Anthem fans even took to chanting Miles' name. Before the next pitch was thrown, Nevaeh heard Emma yell to her brother.

"You can do it, Bro! We're all so proud of you!"

Miles must have heard her as well. When the next pitch was thrown, Miles made contact. The two outs meant that the runner would run on contact. The ball Miles hit did not go far, but it wasn't hit short either. The third baseman and shortstop gave chase toward the outfield as the left fielder ran in. The crowd fell silent. It seemed like no one would be able to catch it, but the shortstop dived and reached as far as he could. The shortstop missed the ball by a hair and the ball dropped onto the grass. The crowd was immediately filled with electricity and signs supporting the Anthem were waving like crazy! The announcer's voice boomed throughout the stadium.

"Miles Saxxby hits a bloop single to short left field! Mr. Saxxby earns himself an RBI and a walk-off win! What a way to win the Championship!"

The rest of the team ran to the field for the celebration. Confetti cannons blasted. Kyle and D.J. took Miles and lifted him onto their shoulders as the confetti fell. Every member of the team was given a T-shirt that read "National Champions – College World Series."

Shortly after the photo opportunity, family and friends joined the players on the field. Morgan, Vinny, Keven, and Rachel ran to Nevaeh and told her how awesome it was to watch her play. When Nevaeh turned, she saw Emma, Miles, and their parents.

"This is the girl I told you about," Emma told them.

"She helped me get a chance to play," Miles said, very excitedly.

Nevaeh reached out her hand and said, "It's a pleasure to meet you."

Mr. Saxxby shook her hand, and said, "You have no idea how much that meant to us!"

Mrs. Saxxby wept, but finally gave Nevaeh a hug and whispered "thank you" into her ear.

Nevaeh told the Saxxby family what an awesome young man Miles was, and that he played baseball like the champion that he was. Nevaeh could see their hearts burst with pride for their son.

When all their parents were gone, Emma told Nevaeh what it all meant. "My Mom said it was a noble thing for you to give up that chance for Miles. They never thought they would get to see him play, but you made it happen. My Mom says that your deed tonight makes you the real hero. From the bottom of our hearts, Nevaeh...Thank You!"

Chapter 32

Once everyone returned home from the college world series, Marcus was summoned to the director's office.

"We called you here today to speak of your deeds during the final game of the college world series," Marion said.

"You may have given Anthem their first National title, but you blatantly disobeyed my command when you let that Saxxby boy hit," George said.

Marcus looked confused. "Please, cut to the chase. Why are we all here?"

"Mr. Hammerhorn has demanded that we reevaluate you, and consider an alternate coaching option," Marion said.

George smiled. "It is with great pleasure that I dismiss you from your position as head co..."

"...Excuse me, Mr. Hammerhorn, but I was not finished speaking," Marion said curtly. "After witnessing Mr. Fjord's coaching skills firsthand, and watching you make a fool of yourself, the other directors held a private meeting to discuss not only your proposal but you as well. At first, I dismissed your actions as being simple frustration, but once I heard you use deplorable words to refer to one of our students, I knew Miss Bennet was correct."

"Correct about what?" George demanded.

"That you're a grumpy old man." Marion lifted her hand as George tried to speak. "The other directors and I discussed both your proposal to replace Mr. Fjord and you. We have come to a decision on both matters. Mr. Fjord will remain as our head baseball coach. As for you, Mr. Hammerhorn, the directors and I have elected to replace you with someone that we feel better suits for what Anthem University stands for."

"And who has replaced ME?" George Hammerhorn demanded.

"That would be me," Coach Kozlowski said, as he entered the room.

George said nothing, and sat there "catching flies", with his mouth opened widely.

"Mr. Hammerhorn, you are dismissed!" Marion Fragnoli said.

George gathered up his belongings and left through the double oak doors. Coach Kozlowski sat in George's chair and graciously accepted to serve Anthem University as one of their new directors.

EPILOGUE

"Morgan! Vinny! Emma! Miles! Rachel!" And a "come here" sign to Keven. "Hurry up! The draft is about to begin," Nevaeh yelled as she sat in front of her television at home. Grandma & Grandpa were there to commemorate this electrifying moment, as well.

"For the last four years, I managed to make it to every one of your games," Morgan said. "Do you really need to yell? I'm not going to miss this!"

"I still can't believe you declared for the MLB draft. My girlfriend is going to be a pro!" Vinny said smiling.

"I might not even get drafted; Coach Fjord convinced me to declare," Nevaeh said.

"Oh, oh, quiet! It's starting," Morgan said.

As the Major League Baseball draft began, the commissioner of baseball gave a speech about the history of the game, and what it meant to play in the majors. After his speech, he announced the order of picks, and a local artist sang The National Anthem. The first ten picks of the draft belonged to the following teams.

(1) Baltimore Orioles

(2) Texas Rangers

(3) New York Mets

(4) Seattle Mariners

(5) Houston Astros

(6) Boston Red Sox

(7) Oakland Athletics

(8) Los Angeles Dodgers

(9) New York Yankees

(10) Washington Nationals

As the ten-minute timer started ticking for Baltimore, everyone sat on the edge of their seat.

"How cool would it be if you were drafted first?" Emma asked Nevaeh.

"I don't even think I'll get drafted," she replied.

"Jackie Robinson probably didn't think he would break the color barrier, but he did," Morgan said. "There's no reason why you can't break the gender barrier.

With five minutes left on the timer, an alert sounded, and the words "Trade Alert" appeared in bright red letters.

"The Baltimore Orioles have traded their pick to the New York Yankees," the voice on the TV said.

A new ten-minute timer started clicking. When the timer reached nine minutes, another alert sounded and the words, "The pick is in," appeared on the screen.

"Wow! That was quick," Vinny said.

Shortly after, the owner of the New York Yankees, Hal Steinbrenner made his way onto the stage.

"With the first pick in the Major League Draft...the New York Yankees select...Catcher, Nevaeh Bennet, Anthem University!" Morgan, Rachel, Keven, Vinny, Emma, Miles & Nevaeh went wild, screaming with excitement. Grandma & Grandpa were holding hands and crying with joy! Mrs. Bennet stood in the archway of their kitchen, pork chops in the oven, reflecting on her husband's success, with tears rolling down her cheeks. She was so very proud of her daughter, Nevaeh. After all, she is her father's daughter...

Baseball Terminology

RBI – Runs Batted In

ERA - Earned Run Average

Double Play - When two outs are made in a single play.

Triple Play – When three outs are made in a single play.

Single - When a player gets a base hit.

Double - When the player hits and reaches second.

Triple – When a player hits and reaches third.

Steal – When a player advances on a pitch.

Pop Up – A ball that is hit high into the air.

Bloop – A ball that is hit, that falls in for a hit, when it shouldn't have.

Full Count – 3 balls, two strikes

Foul ball – A ball that passes the foul line, before passing 1st or 3rd base.

Sac Fly – A ball that is hit, and caught for an out, but a player tags and advances (sacrifice)

Tag – When a ball is caught, the player tags the base they are on and attempts to advance.

Sac Bunt – Sacrifice bunt. Meant to advance runner (batter is out)

Suicide Squeeze – A runner on third steals home as the batter bunts.

Pick Off Attempt – Pitcher throws to base with a runner on, attempts to tag them out (check)

Tag Play – When a runner is not forced to run, they must be tagged to be out.

Force Play – When a player is forced to run, the opposing team only needs to touch the base.

Loaded Bases – A runner on 1st, 2nd, and 3rd.

Grand Slam – A homerun when the bases are loaded.

Retire The Side – The pitcher got 3 consecutive outs.

Error – When a fielder makes a mistake resulting in a run, for failed out.

Save – A closing pitcher ends the game when the other team is threatening to score.

Sweep / Swept – When one team wins every game in a series.

Balk – When a pitcher makes an illegal movement, advancing the baserunner by one base.

Ground Rule Double – The ball is hit and lands in fair territory, but rolls, or bounces out of play. (A runner can only advance two bases.

E + # - Error designated to play by # (E6, E3, E9, etc.)

Pitcher = #1		2nd Base = #4
	Left Field = #7	
Catcher = #2		Shortstop = #5
	Center Field = #8	
1st base = #3		3rd Base = #6
	Right Field = #9	

About the Author

R.E.M. Holland is a former educator who specialized in writing, journalism, and broadcasting. He is an avid New York Yankees and Buffalo Bills fan. Holland is an advocate for diversity and inclusion. He is a former resident of Upstate New York but now resides in South Carolina where he focuses full-time on his writing.

Made in the USA
Columbia, SC
16 September 2024

42296297R00130